Peter Tork

Words of Wisdom From A.A. to ZEN

Peter Tork

Words of Wisdom From AA to ZEN

M.H. Salter

Copyright © 2024 M.H. Salter

Published by Daytime Moon Publishing, South Australia
Edited by M.H. Salter
Front Cover Photo by Jackie Ricciardi
Back Cover Photo by Nurit Wilde

eBook ISBN: 978-0-9925267-9-5
Print Book ISBN: 978-0-9925267-8-8

All rights reserved. This book, or any parts thereof may not be reproduced in any fashion without the written permission of the publisher. The quotes contained within this book are the sole thoughts and opinions of Peter Tork. The author is not claiming copyright to his words.

For Shelly
Always the Jones to my Tork

I'll love you this year
I'll love you next year
and then forever

Foreword 9
Introduction 15
Tork About Abuse 21
Tork About Addiction 29
Tork About Anxiety 41
Tork About Autobiography 45
Tork About the Blues 47
Tork About Books 51
Tork About Cancer Journey 55
Tork About Childhood 69
Tork About Community-ism 75
Tork About Davy Jones 79
Tork About Death 89
Tork About Despair 91
Tork About Education 97
Tork About Facing Morbidity 105
Tork About Forgiveness 109
Tork About Freedom 111
Tork About Happiness 113
Tork About How to do Life 119
Tork About Inspiring Stuff 127
Tork About Loneliness 133
Tork About Love 139
Tork About Michael Nesmith 143

Tork About Micky Dolenz 151

Tork About Money 157

Tork About The Monkees 163

Tork About Music 181

Tork About Parenthood 193

Tork About Peace 197

Tork About Peter Thorkelson 203

Tork About Prejudice 217

Tork About Politics 219

Tork About Possessions 223

Tork About Purpose 227

Tork About Regret 233

Tork About Relationships 235

Tork About Sex 245

Tork About Self-Worth 253

Tork About the Sixties 261

Tork About Sobriety 271

Tork About Spirituality 283

Tork About Trust 295

Tork About Wisdom 297

Tork About Zen 299

Tork About Zhe End… 305

Acknowledgements 309

References 311

Foreword

In December 2007 my husband John and I were driving to Alabama from New Mexico. We'd just finished a winter visit with family on Isleta Pueblo, the Native American reservation he was from, south of Albuquerque. With John at the wheel, we motored I-40 through Oklahoma as a light snow began to fall. Staring out the window at the white flakes fluttering around us I suddenly had an idea — one that popped out of seemingly nowhere, or that amorphous place where ideas reside until they somehow get our attention.

I pulled my computer out of my backpack and composed an e-mail to Peter Tork, because this sudden epiphany had everything to do with him. Peter and I had become friends some years before when I interviewed him for a Japanese magazine. We'd hit it off and formed a lasting friendship that involved long (often serious, occasionally silly) conversations and memorable trips to near and far-flung places. I would visit him in California and later Connecticut, and he visited me at my home in Atlanta.

I loved my internet mobile hotspot (new in those days before our cell phones simplified all communication) because although we were zipping down an interstate it allowed me to immediately send this email telling Peter I had an idea I wanted him to consider. I asked him to call me before Christmas.

That idea was the advice column "Ask Peter Tork."

The notion of The Monkees' multi-instrumentalist writing an advice column wasn't so far-fetched. Peter was a thinker, a reader, open-minded and generous with his talent, his time, and — as I'd noticed from traveling with him as he met friends and fans alike — generous with advice if someone had an issue they wanted to talk about. It didn't matter if he'd known the person-with-a-problem for an hour or his whole life.

An example of this — once in upstate New York, on tour with his band, Shoe Suede Blues — Peter and I met up with a group of people for a late-night meal at an all-night diner. The table was full of folks I didn't know, but Peter knew some of them, which wasn't unusual. He had friends in just about every corner of the country and being on the road with him would often include a blur of friendly faces as we went from state to state. At one point, the conversation focused on a young fan sitting near us. She looked to be just out of her teens and shared how she wanted to become a photographer, but her parents insisted she go to college to do something "sensible." They didn't dig the idea of their child being a photographer, at all, and refused to pay for her education unless she did as they asked. Peter didn't hesitate. He told her to become a photographer if that's what she wanted and not to listen to her parents.

She seemed startled, intrigued and a bit relieved. Here was an adult — pop star Peter Tork, no less — telling her to follow her passion and talent, and ignore her parents' concerns about her future. I smiled as I focused on my salad. This was *so* Peter. He was certain about one formula in the universal equation — use your head when you must but follow your heart.

Peter was also a coin-flipper if an occasion called for it.

A passionate follower of the Tao Te Ching, he would carry a Taoist (I Ching) coin in his pocket, or sometimes an AA coin, and if he was ever unsure about a situation — big, small, or seemingly indifferent — there would be no dithering. He would call heads or tails (even though the coins didn't have the standard sides like moneyed coins do) and whatever came up, that's what he'd do. He did this once when we were trying to decide if we wanted to stay at a crowded restaurant and wait for a table or foot it out and find another eatery.

Coin flip. Heads. We left and found another place to dine.

Peter was a communal soul who cared deeply about his family, his friends, his bandmates (even when they were quarreling) and humanity overall. Both an idealist and an optimist, he was the rare pop star who was often more interested in something besides himself. He was one of the most unpretentious people I've ever known, and his acceptance of the human condition was wide.

Peter was aware of his own foibles and biases and probably keen to yours as well.

If I asked (and sometimes when I didn't) he would offer me gentle advice that could pierce my gloom on any given day with a lighthearted sureness that right thought preceded right action, and balance didn't in any way suck.

Two months following the email I sent from that snowy Oklahoma highway, I put out a press release announcing "Hey, Hey, He's An Advice Columnist" heralding the debut of "Ask Peter Tork" where fans could write in and ask their favorite Monkee for his advice on life, love, relationships, or just his thoughts on show business and the world around us, two things he was intimately acquainted with. I was surprised how easily he agreed to do it and how fully he embraced it.

I shouldn't have been surprised. It was a natural extension of Peter's caring for community and his life's journey to enhance his emotional intelligence and get his own questions answered. He was a person who fully, even eagerly, offered what and who he was, for better (usually) or worse (occasionally). His values might not be your values — after all, this was a quintessential hippie with a socialist bent and a taste for the movable feast — but Peter held no harm or hate in his heart and how many people can honestly say that? He lived and spoke with a frankness that was both delightful and sometimes got him into sticky trouble, as blatant honesty will.

Peter had an admirable ability to circle back after troublesome times and succinctly, methodically, settle the waters, or, if the occasion called for it, simply carry on with a calm that belied any former conflict. He could dislike someone and still speak highly of their good qualities. He carried contradictions easily. Grudges were not his specialty.

I once asked him about what I saw as this amazing ability, for surely one of the hardest things humans grapple with is forgiveness of others or oneself. Moving forward after difficult patches. Navigating regret.

He answered my question with a question.

"Do you want to be *right*," he asked me, "or do you want to be *happy*?"

"I want to be *both*," I answered stubbornly.

Peter, in his wisdom, wanted to be happy. He preferred *you* be happy too.

It's sad to me that Peter is not here to write this foreword. As the only Monkee who didn't publish or write his autobiography (he attempted it once, before abandoning it on principle) he would enjoy this book, I know.

Peter Halsten Thorkelson embraced the world and found the philosophy that worked for his time here on earth. He was a generous soul who wanted to share everything he was and everything he learned. Peter knew you didn't keep the good stuff to yourself.

So he didn't.

Therra Cathryn Gwyn

New Mexico, 2024

Peter Tork: From AA to ZEN

Introduction

This book saved my life.

I've been working on another project for a few years now — *For Pete's Sake: The Peter Tork Biography* (Working Title) — and during the time of researching for that book, my marriage broke down, I sought refuge in too much Pinot Gris, and I underwent a spiritual awakening, ego death, and complete re-evaluation of the meaning of life.

Yeah, it's been a time.

One of Peter's life mottos was to be a hero unto yourself. He was able to remain a hero unto himself after many, many hardships, through which most of us would never be able to see as positives. But *he* did.

So while "being lifed", I kept hearing Peter's words of wisdom: *Be a hero unto yourself. Don't quit before the miracle. Get help, get help, get help.*

Although his advice had not been directed at me specifically, it still applied, it still helped me, it still put me back on my path.

And that's when I *knew* that this needed to be a book unto itself. It could get Peter's words into the hands of others who might be wandering through life a little aimlessly. It could be a guiding light for others, the way it had been for me.

It is no secret that Peter loved to give advice. This is obvious by the time and thought he put in to answering questions for his "Ask Peter Tork" column, and "Peter Sez" on his Official Peter Tork Facebook Page. In a 2010 interview, when asked what gives him the most satisfaction, he replied: *"The most satisfaction in life everyday comes from being useful. I've been working really hard, gaining a lot of understanding, and when somebody else can use it, I'm a happy camper."* I feel this book is a vehicle to allow Peter, even now, to continue to inspire and help others.

If there's someone in the world struggling with addiction and they can read this book and decide to change their path, I believe he will be a happy camper. If there's someone in the world who has been diagnosed with an illness and can, because of Peter's journey, handle their own journey with grace and humour, then he'll be a happy camper. If, through these pages, people can be inspired to pick up an instrument or put on a Peter Tork song and be transported in the same way he was every time he stepped on stage, then he'll be a happy camper.

The quotes in these pages come from his advice column, "Ask Peter Tork", posts he made on his official Facebook page, personal emails direct from Peter, himself, as well as interviews and other sources ranging from 1966 right up until February 2019, just two days before he passed away.

I have compartmentalized his words — mostly un-edited, un-filtered and un-salted — into relevant alphabetized topics. Need help with your marriage? Go to that section. Been diagnosed with an illness? Find out ways to deal. Want to know what Davy Jones was *really* like? Ask Peter Tork. Just need some daily motivation? Flip open to a random page and palm what little pearl is meant for you in that moment. Use his words as your daily meditation.

Please know, whatever your situation, you don't need to do it alone.

If you need it, get help, get help, get help.

Remember to be a hero unto yourself.

And don't quit before the miracle.

With love and understanding,

Melanie Hyland Salter

Peter Tork: From AA to ZEN

Here are my ripostes. I hope they aren't reposts… get it? OK, maybe I'm too hip for the room, but it was wortha try!

As I reread them, I kinda think I'm onto something in at least a couple of cases.

Tell me what you think. Lavish me with praise.

Or both… Heheheh

I do have some ideas. Take what you can use (however little) and leave the rest.

Incidentally, everybody knows this is just my opinion right? I'm not speaking for anybody else. I got a lot of this stuff *from* other people, but I'm not saying it for other people, I'm saying it for *myself.*

~Peter Tork

Tork About Abuse

The characteristic that I have the most trouble with in other people is abusiveness. Loud abusiveness. That one stops me cold, I don't know how to cope with that.[1]

*

It might help, just a bit in the meantime, to consider that bullies are terribly insecure persons who have no clue that their troubles are their own, and must act out on everybody else because otherwise the pressures in their heads would cause them to explode. This doesn't make your memories of your early life any easier, much, but it may just lessen your own pressure, just a bit.

I hope so, anyway.[2]

*

My first response is that your history of bad treatment at the hands of those in a place to diminish you might reflect a phase of your early life. Could this be so? Could you have a history in your youth of being belittled by parents, uncles and aunts, older siblings, etc.? Because one of the things I am sure of is that if so, *you will unconsciously seek out situations that remind you of those early years*. It's a nasty habit that just about everybody has, to some extent. This means that until you deal with the childhood issues, you will not be able to avoid putting yourself in harm's way again and again.

I urge you to begin the work of psychological and spiritual liberation from the burdens of your youth (as I believe would turn out to be the case).

I also hasten to add that it is not the childhood situations themselves which are (or would be) the problem. It is your carrying the lessons your poor young self learned back then that matters.

Along some of the same lines, though, and maybe more to the point right now, is that you are under no obligation to sit still if you do get abuse. Don't stand for it, and don't permit there to be a second incident. If you get a snide comment, challenge the commenter instantly, and demand satisfaction. If none is forthcoming, complain to the leader, and if you still get no support, leave.

You're not obliged to be where you're not appreciated under any circumstances whatever. I'm sure of this.[3]

*

Please know that you most certainly won't stop the bullies' picking on you by giving up the program. They have their reasons, and nothing you can do is likely to change their attitude. (You may be able to stop their bullying you if you can get the help from the counselors and administration of your school(s). Have you asked them for help? Perhaps even the law can help.)

If you can't make serious changes in your situation, then you might be in for a hard few years. (On the other hand, your bullies might lose interest at any time.) At your age, it may come to be an overwhelming burden, and you may not be able to keep it up. If you can, of course, your rewards will be great; a college degree at 18? Can't beat that! Think what you can do with it. You can practically write your own ticket. Freedom!

But this above all: if your well-being is threatened, you must take care of yourself first. There is almost no situation that warrants putting future situations over your present safety. If you can find a way to avoid being at risk at the hands of your tormentors without giving up your program, well and good. But your *present* safety and sanity come before your *future*.[4]

*

I am sad to say that I have very little help for you at the moment. I urge you to stick with your domestic violence classes, and to keep applying what you learn there. I urge you, too, to tell your group of the emotional abuse which is being heaped upon you. It won't make everything all right. I seriously doubt that *anything* will, at least in the near future, but you never know where the help is going to come from, and there's *always* hope.

Meanwhile, if [the abuser] won't leave you alone, you may have a case against him at law for harassment, which then can lead to restraining orders against his coming near your home or your person, or calling you on the phone. There will be the sticky matter of visitation with your other son, but that can be dealt with.[5]

*

I'm not sure I understand. Are you saying your son is abusive [to you and your daughter]? If so, get him out of there! If he's too young to go off on his own, then you have no choice but to throw him on the mercy of whatever family agencies may be near. If he's old enough to go out on his own, he must be sent packing. You don't have to allow abusiveness in your life. I know it sounds harsh, but if you don't get rid of him, he'll bring the whole family down, and you won't be helping him! Honest! I honestly do understand how difficult this is for you, but as I see it you have one *bad* and one *catastrophic* choice. Which will it be?

I'm sorry. But first things first: remove the source of abuse. You have yourself and your daughter to take care of.

BTW, it's possible your son is schizophrenic, about which you can do nothing on your own. I repeat, you can't be of any use to him if this is the case. You can't be of any use to him if he's suffering from a wide range of mental health issues. Save yourself and your daughter, and you'll then be in a better position to be of use to him.[6]

*

All I can say is, if your brother can't be relied upon to treat others as himself, then he can't be relied upon. There is no shame in protecting yourself, your loved ones, and your worldly possessions from this guy's access. It does not mean you don't love him, and it does not mean you have to have a hard heart in your chest. Just don't confuse love for mushiness. You do him, yourself and others, no favors by being lax in your protection of yourself and your loved ones. Nobody's perfect, and it's worse than foolish not to be clear-eyed about other people. It's downright dangerous. Too many people I know of believe that if they treat others as though these others were saints, they will be protected, somehow, from harm. Their confusion when they get bitten in the ass is painful to see.

You might get considerable comfort and support from the people at Al-Anon (look them up under Al-Anon Family Groups) or ACA (called Adult Children of Alcoholics, but really for the adult children of any dysfunctional parents). Meantime, be of good cheer, love your brother — at a distance! — and go about your business. He will come to his senses or he won't, and it has nothing to do with you, so don't get your boxers in a knot about it.[7]

*

You didn't indicate very clearly whether the abuse is still going on. But if it is: do you have any way to get to any place other than that house? Any way at all. Go to a relative's house. Throw yourself on the mercy of the child welfare system. I can't tell you to run away from home if you don't have a safe place to go to, but if you do have one, even one that isn't perfect but better, go there. The first order of business is to get you out of that abusive situation. I know you'll feel like you're deserting your mom and brother if you leave, but if I read you right, you have no power in that household as it is, and you'll have even less if you can't get out.

You also didn't say your age. If you're in your early teens, you will only be able to escape. If you're in your later teens, you might consider going for emancipation.

Meanwhile, don't worry about your friends. If they don't have a grasp of the seriousness of your situation, they can't be of much help, and that means, by my definition, that they aren't friends at all. You have a very tough row to hoe, my friend, and you need all the help you can get, and you don't have much time for those who can't be on your side in working ways.

I hasten to add that you *can* do this. You can assemble a life of integrity and strength. You won't be able to do it gracefully, and it won't be easy, but if you can ask for help — and that means from whatever Higher Power you know, as well as whatever earthly agencies are available — you can get through all this. You will find friends who are on your side, and you will grow to be a strong person who will bring integrity and bravery to the situation in your home of origin, and thus to the world at large.

If, by some happy other chance, your mom's husband isn't there any more, well, then you're certainly better off. But the previous paragraph still applies. You're going to need help to grow, and those who can't help aren't worth much of your time, etc., etc., etc.[8]

*

Prison was like burning off some left over high school karma. I had been dodging bullies all the time in high school and I finally learned to face that. I couldn't dodge them [in prison], had to learn to face them. You know, the bad boys are there, and there was nowhere to go, so you've got to learn to cope, face to face, and I did.

I learned to deal on a human basis. That's what it came down to. [At school] I didn't have the tools to face guys on a human basis, I had no human tools, and I got those together, and then I got this jail thing and I had to deal with these guys. It's like the line from the Beach Boys song, "I Get Around", "The bad guys know us and they leave us alone." That's what it is, the bad guys knew me and they left me alone, that was all there was to it.

I just said, "I'm not going to play your game; I'm not going to kowtow. No, I don't want to have anything to do with you. No, I am not interested in getting in the middle of your game either. We'll just leave each other alone. Everything will be okay." Fine. End of story.

And that's what it took. And that's what it was for, karmically speaking you know, in that kind of transcendental thing.[9]

*

Certainly I learned something from those who hurt me, but it was on the order of learning not to touch a red-hot electric stove. Useful, you know, but totally limited to: "Don't go near that again." I've learned far more from sympathetic people, folks who were on my side.

I ask you: which is more valuable, knowing to not touch a hot stove, or knowing how far from a fire to sit to stay warm? I mean to say, they're both valuable, but the one is broader and deeper than the other.[10]

Tork About Addiction

Alcohol was my compensatory habit, numbing my feelings of not being truly noticed or regarded. Of course, it really only served to take me *away* from my own life, not make it better.[11]

*

I think the best teller of the disease — there's two good tells, I think. One of them is: do you drink when it's against your better interest to do so? And when the information is there that lets you know?

And the other is: personality changes. And I used to see my father with personality changes.[12]

*

There never was a time when I couldn't drink. I was always allowed to have wine with the parents, and I was always allowed to drink a little if that's what I wanted it for. However I was not aware of the disease or the syndrome of alcoholism until I was in my mid-thirties. Although I have a friend who remembers personality changes in my twenties. But I don't remember them. I only had one blackout that I can place. I'm sure there were others.[13]

*

Did the entertainment industry drive me to drink? No, of course not! The kind of personality trends that sent me to entertainment were there long before I got into trouble with any chemistry whatsoever.

I mean, there never was a time I *couldn't* drink. My parents let me drink wine if I wanted with dinner, or a sip of a cocktail or a bit of beer — they never cared — and I never got too deeply into it when I was young. But it's pretty clear that alcoholics have a curve to their disease, their syndrome, that is basically not affected by life or by anything else. It's genetic, it's in their bones, and I guess my curve hadn't taken over me. I didn't even realize I was in trouble until my mid to late thirties. One or two friends of mine knew I was in trouble before that, but not many.[14]

*

One of the features of alcoholism has to do with isolation. You feel that you're better than everyone else, you feel that you're worthy of *anybody* else's company; it's called Arrogant Doormat Syndrome. And I had it. There's an awful lot of abnormal pressures in that [sixties] rock scene.

I truly believe that some of the characteristics of the disease I had as a child. Some of them were exacerbated by show biz. On the other hand, I might not have gotten into show biz if I hadn't been this way, so they fed each other.[15]

*

I can't ascribe my alcoholism to fame, I can more easily do it the other way around. One of the things about alcoholics, to the extent that I've been able to make any observations, is that we are either above the crowd or below it – or both at the same time. The reason you shoot to be above is because you feel below, and the reason you feel below is because you're not part of, never one of the guys. You envy the people who seem to have a certain contentment. The character makeup that sent me into pop stardom is the same character makeup that sought to anesthetize myself with chemistry. I found that it was not until I put all of that chemistry behind me that I began to get back in touch with my place in the human scheme of things.[16]

*

If you're fixed on the notion that an orgy is going to fulfill you, and one doesn't do it, you're going to try a hundred. If orgies don't do it, maybe drugs will. Like the fixated person I was then, I went from one thing to another. I had to try *everything*: flower power, dope, orgies, fast cars.

In the beginning drinking was a lot of fun, I have some memories of things that I did drunk that I never would have done sober, that I guess I always sort of wanted to do. But drinking isn't selective. It doesn't let you do exactly what you want to do and keep you from doing the things you don't want to do. Furthermore, at a certain point, and I think with certain personality types, it's addictive. You find you cannot drink moderately any longer. It finally reached a point with me where it was obvious that I was going to die if I kept up with it. I was never hospitalized, but I could see the path. I realized I was out of control.[17]

*

Basically, I avoided facing my life as well as I could. The more I did, the more I drank, the more I avoided my life. And the pressures of your life are going to build up on you. And the reason that a lot of this stuff is addictive is that you brush away some modest worry with a glass of something, and then the next day, that worry — Tuesday's worry *and* Thursday's worry —

comes in together. It takes *two* glasses of beer to shove off Tuesday's and Thursdays worry. Then comes Sunday's worry down the throat, and the other two haven't been taken care of, it takes *three* glasses of beer. And that's why it's cumulative, and addictive in the sense that's why I found my disease to be addictive: it was about fending off life. And the great, incredible blessing is that you do not get more than you can handle. Or to put it another way, your denial is still functioning, if it's too big, you don't know.[18]

*

And while we're on the subject of strange arithmetic, for me, when it came to drinking, one less than two choices, is *no* choice. If I didn't have the power to refuse, I had *no* choice. There wasn't *one* choice, it was *none*. If I started, I kept on going. Usually until — I mean if I had enough presence of mind to make it to bed then, that's about all I had.[19]

*

I would get drunk and behave badly, and it wouldn't happen again for months and months and months, and everybody thought, "Oh well, Peter's just had a few too many."

And it didn't happen all the time, and like the man says, I didn't get into trouble every time I picked up a drink, but every time I got into trouble, I'd been drinking.

But if your bouts of trouble are months and months apart, as they were with me, nobody notices the pattern until you come back and say, "I'm not drinking anymore." And they go, "Oh, that explains such and such." You know?

A lot of my friends who weren't drinking noticed more in hindsight: "Now that you tell me this, that makes more sense than it did before." And their memories suddenly make more sense. And that kind of thing.

So no. Nobody said to me, "Peter, you're playing in traffic and you're going to get hit."[20]

*

From about the time that I began to become aware that I was having some trouble with alcohol, until the time that I was able to come in — which was a matter of three to five years — during that time I began to watch myself.

I began to notice how many times I planned to have two beers and went to bed with the spins under the influence of nine, wondering how'd I get there?

I began to notice the number of times I had to apologize each morning for the behaviors of the night before.

I began to notice, whether I meant to or not, how many times I went to bed with the spins, and debating with myself: was I gonna try to fall asleep behind all this, or was I just going to go to the bathroom and stick my finger down my throat? I did that a lot.[21]

*

And one day, I looked at a can of beer in my hand and I had a shock. What I realized was that I hadn't *asked* for it. Up 'til then, as far as I knew, every single time that I had a beer, I had said, "Gee, a beer would be great right now," or, "I think I'll have a beer," or, "Hey, I have an idea, I'll have a beer." And this one time, I suddenly saw that I had had no mental construction of any kind. I had grabbed a beer absolutely automatically.

I've heard this before, in several different orders, but the one that makes sense to me is: *the man takes the drink, the drink takes the man, the drink takes the drink.* And it got to that point. I was just a vehicle for alcoholism's will. I was a servant of alcoholism.[22]

*

My actual bottom was that I was in a dark and gloomy apartment, and I had a beer in my hand, and I suddenly saw that I hadn't had any mental construct of indicating that I wanted it, you know? At no point did I go, "Gee, I'd love a beer," or, "A beer would be great right now." I just suddenly noticed that it had been *automatic*, and the scales fell from my eyes at that point. And I had been fighting it. I had been understanding that I was in trouble and struggling with it, one way or another for three, or five years before that. But it wasn't until then that I saw that I was completely out of control. Nothing that I could do could have any serious effect, and I basically despaired of any rescue.

But I actually had had word of what to do and how to… I was able to give it up, and I haven't had a drink since, and that was over twenty years ago with the alcohol — although I did keep smoking pot. I will be totally clean and dry twenty years come January, God willing.[23]

*

My opinion on marijuana is that it should be, if not exactly legalized, at least decriminalized. There remains a certain attitude among the ruling class that seeks to punish rather than include. As for myself, I recommend not smoking it (or putting it in brownies, etc.). When I'm with anyone who smokes it, they go away, and I'm alone whether they're there or not. I believe it delays life, as, I believe, does alcohol. You could not have convinced me of this when I was smoking it, but I am sure of that now. But I am also certain that those who want to smoke it will, and I see no public interest in spending valuable police and court time on the matter. Nor do I see any public interest in coercing people into getting on with their lives; they just rebel all the harder, as I did myself, and it was actually a useful time in my life, in the long run.[24]

*

You get on a vicious cycle, and you don't know how you're going to get off. Because you're certainly convinced that if you try to get off, you will be instantly and magically propelled into poverty and fear and ignorance and loathing and screaming gibbering terror. And you can't get over that without somebody to guide you through the baby steps it takes to get from there to here, or here to there.

It's taken me all these years to find people who will give me the guidance and the baby steps. This is something I'm sure you cannot do alone. The worst part about all of the greed and loneliness and the addictions is that they can foster aloneness, making it harder to get the help it takes to get off the wheel.

Incidentally, this is the wheel that the Buddhists and the Hindus talk about when they're saying the "wheel of karma." You can't get off it, the squirrel wheel, you run around and around. That's the image. You can't get off it without help, and you can't ask for help when you're on the wheel, because you're so sure there is no help, that to ask for help is to leave yourself open to worse ridicule and more nastiness, so it's really very, very difficult to get off the wheel. But everybody I know who's gotten off that wheel is grateful beyond the power of words to express. Nobody says, "Gee, I wish I was still chasing money or women or drinking or smoking dope," that kind of thing.

It used to be sex, drugs and rock & roll. Now it's sex, sushi and the blues.[25]

*

By and large, yeah, at least it felt like a party, you know. It's like, I look back now… and I told my son — he's been doing some stuff — and I was able to say to him, "Listen, I can't tell you, 'Don't do this, don't do that,' because I did it all — and lot's more, too! But I *can* tell you that I wish I had done a great deal *less*."

When I look now at my life, and the satisfactions I have from the blues band, and from a clean and sober life, if I had known then what I know now I would've dumped all of that chemistry junk a long time previously!

You know, one of the things about chemical abuse is that it affects the centers of your brain which would have enabled you to know that what you're doing is stupid. But you don't know that you're stupid because that part of your brain is shut down by the chemistry. So you go around thinking that you're having a great time, and you don't get enough input until it gets really drastic. I mean, it wasn't until I was snarling at my wife and children out of the blue, and waking up with hangovers. I gave my son a haircut and my hand was shaking, and I said, "Must be too much coffee." And my wife took me aside afterwards and said, "No, you were drinking a lot last night. It's the shakes." And I had to say, "My god, you're probably right!"

And it took a lot of really graphic physical evidence for me to *get* that I had long overdrawn at the bank, you know. I was *way* in deficit.[26]

*

There are two kinds of pain. One is the pain of growing up. The other is the pain of refusing to do so. To my mind, the first is better because although it's infinitely more difficult to deal with, at least it changes. It somehow gets better.

Looking back now, I realize I was compulsive. And that comes from the lie that you "have to do everything yourself". Making it. And you can't make it without the support system of other people. I think this whole business we're into now about glorifying the individual is a temporary historical aberration: that you *can't* ask for help, that there is *no* sense of community. Anyway, at the end of the long road, the chemistry backfired. It was like being totally aphasic. Conversations which, when I started with drugs, seemed intelligent, articulate and enlightening, at the end became disjointed.

On the road, I would reward myself for not getting blitzed before a performance by getting blitzed after it. I'd make promises to myself at home and then the minute I got back on the road, the controls came off and I was right back where I started from. When you're in that condition, issues of will become very fuzzy. I realized I had a choice. Either a dull life or no life at all. Amazingly, life straight and sober has turned out to be a delight. Now I'm blitzed on natch.[27]

*

My experience indicates that there is almost nothing you can do directly about a drug addict and/or alcoholic. If you find that one such is making your life crazy, you — repeat *you* — should start attending al-anon meetings. It turns out that people who are all up in an alcoholic's life have a mirror disorder of their own, and the attention they pay the addict/alcoholic is attention they are *not* paying their own lives. If you are one of these, get thee thence![28]

*

Alcoholics are a ferociously defiant bunch, and it's likely that the more you try to do to get him dry, the more intensely he will drink "at" you. You have only one realm where you have any control, and that's your own life. Get to a half-dozen Al-Anon meetings and see if being there doesn't help put your life into a different frame. Your friend is in the hands of his own reality, and there's probably no room for you.[29]

*

According to my best information, AA is not the only way to go, nor does it have any tools or methods not available elsewhere. The only thing is, AA's particular combination of tools and methods has by far the best record of helping people who describe themselves as you do to stop drinking. I can tell you from my experience that shyness, fierce independence and position are no excuses for *not* going. In fact, as far as I'm concerned, the only reason for not going is that you don't want to stop drinking. *Yet*. That's OK, mind you, but if you think alcohol is a problem, then there's no reason not to go to AA other than this: you have a disease, which includes, among its effects, the belief that you don't have a problem. (This isn't quite as far-fetched as it sounds: there are now many recognized diseases which have behavioral and cognitive components. Tourette's and OCD come instantly to mind.)

BTW, believe me, your standing in the community is no impediment to your going to AA. Everyone in there has been where you are, and no one is inclined to make your recovery a matter of public knowledge. After all, they're all in the same boat.

In addition, I can tell you that a self-image of being fiercely independent and a "suck it up and deal with it" kind of person is a strong inducement to avoiding getting help, and probably of no use whatever in overcoming problem drinking. See, use of alcohol, which is habitual and maybe even compulsive, comes from an unease in company, and a sense of not belonging. (This in turn disguises itself as independence.) Alcohol shuts down those parts of the brain which are concerned with these things, so you no longer feel the discomfort. It feels pretty good, actually, but eventually alcohol bites you in the ass, and it overpowers its one-time benefits.

(As for me, well, I will only share with you my understanding that AA members are requested not to divulge their membership at the public level. This, as I understand it, is to keep celebrities from blasting it all over the place that they're sober. What if they fall off the wagon? That wouldn't help anyone.)

So, go! Check it out. You really have nothing to lose. Go for a month before you decide. If it doesn't work, you can try plan B, which I will go into if it comes to that. Let me know.[30]

Tork About Anxiety

I'm sad to hear of your anxieties.

You must realize that there is no earthly reason why these thoughts of future activities should be scary. I underline "earthly" to say that your anxieties can not, rationally, arise from what is normally an *excited* anticipation. Therefore and hence, you have issues.

Don't despair, everybody does, to some extent or another. They can be dealt with. The point is that something is dogging you. I believe, on scant evidence, that it's likely that you have childhood issues that cloud your sense of pleasure at the coming adventure. The other possibility is that you have anxiety disorders stemming from some genetic distraction. Don't freak out here, either. This, too, is treatable.

BUT here's the good news: none of this is fatal. It doesn't even have to be crippling. No matter where it came from, it can be dealt with.

Firstly, you don't have to face the stuff right away. Your anxiety may disappear as you get nearer to it all. In the meantime, and alternatively, you may find the psychological and spiritual counseling it takes to get past this.

I also recommend meditation as a means of calming the soul. My favorite brand of that is Zen, but whatever you prefer you should do.[31]

*

I might ask how you know you have an overwhelming fear of dentists? I know that sounds a bit silly, but a lot of people talk themselves into things just by repeating their story over and over to themselves.

So, try saying to yourself instead, "I have nothing to fear there; I can handle what comes my way. I am in charge of my own attitude."

Say it out loud several times a day, and write it down three times a day, once in the first person, once in the second ("You, [your name], have nothing to fear..." etc.) and once in the third ("[your name] has nothing to fear..."). Particularly do this if you catch yourself trying to remind yourself how you have an overwhelming fear of dentists. Let me know if this helps.

But before I'm done, let me ask you a bigger question, one that won't make any difference for this upcoming visit, but is very important. *Do you panic if you don't have a sense of control?* Because, if so, your problem may be *bigger* than the fear of the dentist. The truth is, you know, we have very little control over people, places and things in the outside world. But if your sense of control is critical to your well-being, then it's time to examine the why's and wherefore's of your underlying belief that the world is actually chaotically threatening. (This notion was probably a very sensible conclusion in your youth, but it's time to get to work on it.)

I had a friend who hated to fly because he got tired holding the plane up from his passenger's seat. Heheheh. In the long run, you know, getting to the bottom of that conviction of chaos is the key to a free life. Get help; you almost certainly can't do it by yourself. Some churches may help, group therapy (one-on-one may not be as effective), finding people who are on your side, that kind of thing will go a long way toward helping you connect with life in all its unexpectedness.[32]

*

The qualities that make all the difference between being laughed *at* and laughed *with* are acceptance and love. It's as simple as that! We know that there are people everywhere who seem to carry hate in their hearts. It's pretty hard to get through to them. But there are many, many more people in the world who have love in their hearts and who like to laugh. And it never hurts to be laughed *with*. All good comedians are laughed *with* because they're loving the audience and the audience is accepting the love that the comedians are giving them.

The handful of people who carry hate and send out hate vibrations only deserve to be pitied because they're missing out on the whole groovy, love-filled happening called *life*!

So, no matter what your secret fear is, if it has to do with people, as most fears do in some way or another, you can apply this solution to it. I know it works because I've proved it with mine. Just zero in on it and ask: "Are they acting toward you out of *love* or out of *hate*?"

If it's out of hate, there's really nothing to fear because hate doesn't really exist — it's only the *absence* of love and you can just feel sorry for them. And realize this: your love can fill their emptiness and win out! And, of course, if they're acting out of love, well, there's *definitely* nothing to fear because then they're with you all the way![33]

Tork About Autobiography

I must say that as the years roll by, I'm less and less inclined to write that autobiography, and I wasn't any too motivated to begin with. You know, it's about the work. I'm a pretty lazy guy. Chances are slim for an autobio.[34]

*

I have thought about writing a book many times. I did start to write one; I wrote about 60 pages and then stopped. You know, I do what I do. I don't know why I don't do what I don't do, particularly.[35]

*

As to my tell-all book, well, I don't believe that's going to happen. Never say never, of course, but I've thought about it off and on for years, and I never seem to sit down to the computer and start writing the thing. Meanwhile, I do make music, and that's where my heart is. These days, it's just about all about the blues.[36]

Tork About the Blues

The blues overtook me at a time I was left without feelings. Before that, I didn't know *how* to do it, or didn't feel I had a *right* to do it, and didn't know if I *could* ever do it.

My experience with the blues when I do it well, is that I am relieved of my trials and tribulations. The blues remove you, for a moment, from everyday worries.

But more importantly, the blues allow people to realize that everyone is struggling through similar situations, building a common reference of understanding.

People might go out later and treat others a little better because they've come to understand we're all having the same kind of problems. Blues isn't about being blue. It's about sadness, women, low life, upbringing, but it is *not* designed to bring you down. Everyone relaxes a little and maybe treats their neighbor a little better. No Monkee business.[37]

*

I must say that I enjoyed The Monkees music myself pretty much in proportion as it was bluesy, with some notable exceptions. ("Pleasant Valley Sunday", my favorite M's single, has very little of the blues to it, to my ear.)

But what it is about the blues, well, I can only tell you that the blues, to some extent or other, has always turned my head around. My folks did have records by The Weavers and Josh White and a few 40's jump swing boogie songs, but the dominant mode for me growing up was classical, and that's what I took when I first took piano. Still, when rock and roll came in, in the 50's, it was the bluesiest of the songs that got me the most. Early Elvis, Little Richard, these were the performers I was drawn to. As I got into folk music for myself toward the end of the 50's and into the early 60's, I didn't have the confidence it took to even *try* the blues.

It's taken me all these years to believe that a) I understand the blues enough socially and emotionally, and b) that I have the technique to play them. A well played blues NOTE, to this day, makes my heart sing. I also had the good fortune to listen to a wonderful blues band every Monday for several years. It was led by a man named Larry Johnson, not the recorded blues player of the same name, but he was good, and he knew the blues backwards and forwards. When I'd walk into that club and the band would strike up, I'd feel my heart relax, time after time. As far as I'm concerned, the blues is not about the blues. That is, the stuff of the blues — abandonment and heartache — those are only the outward show. The blues is really all about: we've all had the blues, and we're all human because of it. It's just that simple. When I hear the blues done right, I know I belong on the face of the earth.[38]

*

I never hear the blues done right but that I don't heave a sigh of relief to remember that the world's all right and that I belong in it.

There's a quality of humanity in the blues for me that pop music doesn't have — at least not very much. It has to do with the beat, and the folks who created it, and their trials and tribulations, reminding me that we all have troubles. Pop music, it seems to me, tries to drown out or distract from the trials of life. The blues tells me that we're all in this together, and that I don't have to pretend to be all right when I'm not.

As to the tunes I choose, I just choose the ones I enjoy, giving preference to originals. That's about it.[39]

*

There's something about blues notes, about blues beat, about the sensibility of the blues, all of those things have always gone really deep for me, deeply into my core someplace. I will tell you I've worked on this question for myself through the last few years and it comes down to this for me: pop music is a distraction, pop music is usually about taking your mind off your troubles, particularly dance music nowadays, disco music and discotheque music is really about pounding — the old joke about, if I stomp on your foot you forget that your finger hurts — something like that I think. But the blues is genuinely *healing* because it works into the issues of recovery, the disease of alcoholism — all the diseases — are diseases of isolation. You go into the disco or you drink (or both) and that for a while successfully removes the insistence of the information that you're all alone. But with the blues in hand you simply are not all alone, you're actually in company. You're the same as everybody else, everybody goes through that, everybody's had the blues. It really is like the white man's disease — "I don't have the blues, I'm fine, I can take care of myself" — that kind of frontier, isolationist attitude, which is incidentally in my opinion bringing the country to wreck and ruin, but that's an outside issue, which I will not pursue any longer.

Point being however, the blues tells me that the fact that I'm sometimes out of whack, and sometimes lost, and feeling a little bit alone, that doesn't make me unique and expellable. If you're feeling lonely or down, "Oh, what are you talking about? You've got no reason; have a drink, you should feel great!" Which is essentially rejection. The rejection of your truth. And the blues tells you, "No man, everybody's been there."

You don't have to drink, but you don't have to pull that — "I'm a man, I can take care of myself" — stuff.

You can just say, "Listen, I'm feeling down, other people are feeling down, it's not a happy place to be is it?"

"No it isn't. I've been there man, I get it."[40]

*

You don't have to have been a black sharecropper to play the blues.

But you do have to have overcome the white man's disease, which is "otherizing" everyone else — distancing yourself from the humanity of anyone who *isn't* you.

Once you overcome that, the only question about playing the blues is whether you *feel* them.

When you catch a good blues groove, it's unlike anything else in this world.[41]

Tork About Books

Well, I read a lot, you know. One of my favorite books right now is *Stranger in a Strange Land*, which is pretty well what the title says. And there's a book called *Book of Changes* [*I Ching: The Book Of Changes*], which is very interesting. I'm doing quite a lot of reading on Eastern religions. It sort of widens my general knowledge and anyway it's a fascinating part of the world — China, India, all that.[42]

*

One of my favorite books now [1968] is *Stranger in a Strange Land* by Robert Heinlein. It's about the orphan child of the first Martian explorers. He grows to twenty-one years of age before he's discovered by the second expedition to Mars which rescues him. He comes back to Earth, having been raised by the Martians — really fascinating![43]

*

Another writer I dig is Theodore Sturgeon, one of the greatest science fiction writers alive today. He visited our set one day and we were all very thrilled. He's a visionary and a mystic, really one of the giant talents of the day. I hope everybody reads him. He wrote a book called *More Than Human* and a lot of other novels and short stories.[44]

*

Zen Mind, Beginner's Mind, by Shunryu Suzuki. It's all about watching your own mind rather than obeying it as though it were the infallible voice of the truth.[45]

*

The Sayings of Buddha (a small, inexpensive book you can find in almost any book store) always rests on the night-table beside my bed. I find that ancient wisdom, meditation and contemplation puts my mind in order and brings me great serenity.[46]

*

This is a book of some of the excerpts of the *Upanishads*. Actually, these are excerpts from ancient Hindu writings. I guess you could say that in a sense they are like the Bible, only they were written many centuries before the old testament. Well, the *Upanishads* are simply but beautifully written. I mean, they are quite easy to understand. You can buy the Mentor pocket edition for about 50 cents.[47]

*

Book recommendations by Peter Tork

- *How to Play the 5-String Banjo* by Pete Seeger
- *Why do I Say Yes When I Need to Say No? Escaping the Trap Of Temptation* by Michelle McKinney Hammond
- *Don't Say Yes When You Want to Say No: Making Life Right When it Feels All Wrong* by Herbert Fensterheim and Jean Baer
- *Games People Play* by Eric Berne
- *Letters to a Young Poet* by Rainer Maria Rilke
- *Tao Te Ching* by Laozi
- *I Ching: The Book Of Changes*
- *Everyday Zen* by Charlotte Joko Beck
- *Think on These Things* by J. Krishnamurti

Tork About Cancer Journey

Author's note:

The below emails and Facebook posts were written by Peter throughout his entire cancer journey, from 2009 until 2019, in order to keep family, friends and fans updated on his progress. They show his upbeat spirit, and his commitment to getting healthy. I hope that his words can inspire anyone who may be going through something similar, or have loved ones who are on that journey themselves.

Don't quit before the miracle.

*

Subject: Doc, I broke my leg in two places! "Well, stay away from those places"

Date: Feb 10, 2009 6:04 PM

Dear, darling diva divine,

I am fine. Nothing new on the doctor front at the moment, but I go into the hospital tomorrow morning for a few hours to have a biopsy, the which they put me under for. Yuk. I have a p.e.t. scan the next day, and I get the definitive diagnosis the following Wednesday. Meanwhile, I am under instructions to speak not at all, or at least very very little, for 3-4 days. Can you imagine? MOI?

Heheheh

Of course, I'll still be able to email, etc., etc., etc., unless I develop a provisional diagnosis of cancer of the fingers.

Unlikely, I'm sure.

*

Subject: Re: Lovin' you long distance!

Date: Feb 11, 2009 8:25 PM

Thanks for your good wishes, babe. As it happens I am in terrific spirits, except when I have to swallow, but even that's not too bad. The thing I was dreading the most was coming out of general, but it was like waking up from a good nap. They sure have improved matters since I was last under anaesthesia (note perfect old-fashioned spelling). Plus the doctor took more off than just what was needed for a biopsy, and that should actually make matters a bit easier. There was more good news; they explored around and about just to see if there were any more suspicious areas, and there are not.

I am most certainly looking forward to your cookies. All of them.

xoxoxo. Lots of them, too.

Moi

*

Subject: my growth…

Date: Friday, February 27, 2009, 8:03pm

Dear friends, romans, countrymen, countrywomen,

I've been struck with some news. It isn't good.

It may not be all that bad, but at the very best it's a nasty little speed bump in the road of life.

I've been diagnosed with a cancer on the tongue.

It's called an adenoid cystic carcinoma, and it's pretty big as these things go — and I *soitenly* wish this one would (Groucho impression).

The (relatively) good news is actually pretty good. There is no sign of metastasis or any other kind of spreading. The treatment plan involves surgery and radiation, which will entail some discomfort for a while, BUT the best (tentative) good news of all is that, barring unhappy, unknown extra developments, the prognosis is for a complete recovery in three months, with (again, barring nasty surprises) *no likely recurrence*. That is, if the surgery is good, and the radiation does its job, and there are no other growths lurking in the microscopic world, *this will not come back*. This is in happy marked contrast to some other cancers where they blast the sucker with radiation, hope for the best, but give you only about a 30% chance of no further developments. This one is in the 90% effective range, better given my rather revolting good health.

The additional good news is, I've been told I may expect to be back to singing and performing in my fabulous blues band by June, when we have a date here on the east coast (Manchester CT to be precise), and I hope thereupon to take up a full schedule of touring, larking about and giving all y'all a hard time, as is my practice and habit.

Meanwhile, I am in disgustingly good spirits. Either that, or I'm in the biggest denial I've ever heard of. I prefer the former view, of course. I mean, what am I going to do, bewail my fate? Hold my breath 'til my face turns blue? Ya, like that'd help.

All of you are important in my world, and I know each and every one of you (with maybe one exception — ok, joke) wishes me well. I feast off your concern, and you have my gratitude for being in my circle all, all in a positive, sometimes even loving, way.

Bless and keep you, every one,

Peter

Email Subject: The Monday Peter Update (From Hallie)
Date: Tuesday, March 10, 2009, 12:16am

Peter says:

"Beloved mob, my color is up, my swelling is down, but my lower lip is swollen, as is my lower chin area — if I tilt my head just so, I look like a gangster from Queens."

But really, folks, his color is up and he is detached from most of the tubes. His spirits are better than yesterday.

When I got to the hospital he was sitting up, now he is sleeping and resting.

Attached is a "before" and "after" picture.

He loves reading your responses, so keep them coming.

Love,

Hallie

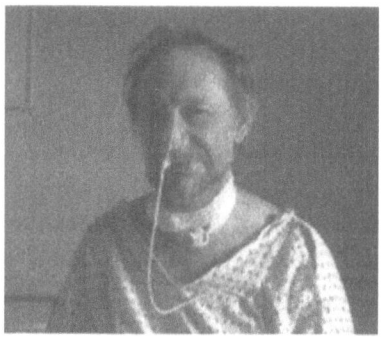

Subject: Inside Story, late edition

Date: Wednesday, March 25, 2009, 11:50pm

Dear friends and otherwise interested parties and extravagant celebrations,

I spoke to "Inside Edition" the other day. On camera... When will it be shown? The answer is, it's ambiguous. The answer is ambiguous, as so many of us are, so very, very often.

Meanwhile, as long as I have your attention:

I went to my dentist — actually, my prosthodontist. What a word! — to see about getting some kind of device in my mouth that would prevent me from sounding more like Daffy Duck than usual (lots more). Trying to get said device into my mouth turned out to be a hassle, so if you see me on the street, please stand well away from the spew of "suffering succotash," and such-like sounds.

Otherwise, as you have probably already discerned, my spirits are back up pretty well. Not that I don't still sleep uncounted hours per day, but I'm reconciled to it, and even exulting in it. Lazy? Not me! I'm in reCOVery from significant SURgery!

Beyond that, there's not much news to report. I'm getting a lot of help with the [maple] syruping, and I wish you-all were here to enjoy the process, and not incidentally, schlep some buckets around and tend the fire. Even without you, or at least without all of you, it looks like there's going to be a nice crop this year. Not what it could have been, of course, but good just the same. Apply for gift bottles, you may get lucky.

Thanks, as always, for your interest. Ttyl8r, as they say... or type... or data entry... or txt... or whatever. Whatever.

Peter

*

Subject: glowing reports

Date: Wednesday, April 8, 2009, 2:17pm

Hey, y'all. All y'all,

I'm writing this on the train back to New Haven after the most recent doctor's appointment. I seem to be doing especially well; when I told the — what? assisting? resident? younger — doctors that my surgery was only a few days more than a month ago, they expressed amazement. Maybe they were playing with me, but it does seem that my unusual constitution is standing me in good stead still.

My good friend Lauren, who it was that booted me into my initial appointment with the medical community — did I say thanks, Lo, and I love you? — called me today to try to warn me off of radiation. It seems that her husband went through some horrendous stuff with radiation after a head-and-neck cancer leaving him without salivary glands among other indignities. Consequently, taking myself in hand, I asked the good doctor about that. What were chances as between radiation and no radiation? Would I be left without salivary glands? The doctor's answer was that there *is* a numerical (statistical) difference between going forth with radiation and without, though he wouldn't give me the real numbers, but he did go on to say that my salivary glands won't be affected, and that the problem with going without radiation is that if I do, and there's a recurrence, it might be vastly more difficult to deal with. Soo, tomorrow (well, today, actually, as it's now hours after I started this little missive) I'll call the radiation doctor and get started with the process. Dr. Shah says six weeks of radiation, and reiterates for me not to cancel my gig in June. So, y'all come to Manchester CT, it's a free gig. Cheer me on and overlook the weak parts — if any, heheh. (Specifics, like time and location, to follow.)

My energy is still generally good, if in short-ish supply and I'm doing some of my singing exercises. Actually, I'm feeling pretty chipper.

Oh, yeah, and I can eat soft solid food now. I'm off the purée diet. I think I'll keep up with the smoothies for breakfast, they're great, but I had salmon, potatoes and broccoli tonight for supper. What fun!

Thanks for your attention, you know it's like mother's milk to me.

*

Subject: update on the kid's progress

Date: Wednesday, April 22, 2009, 11:50pm

I've been getting a lot of emails back from some of you, and been very glad of them, too. I am actually amazed at the response, and the outpouring of support. I haven't been a bit discouraged by those of you who haven't called or written. I know you're busy. It's ok.

It's been a while since I wrote last, and a lot has happened. Susan Boyle, for one. Torture memos from the highest echelons of the last administration for another. Quite a wide spread of events, actually, and that doesn't include my health story, which is actually quite tame by comparison. Really, the reason it's been so long since I last wrote is just that not much has changed with me.

I'm still in recovery from the surgery, though getting better every day. The process on that front has slowed down some, and the changes are relatively minor these days. Generally, I feel pretty good; I'm singing and playing guitar some. I am still numb in lip and tongue (not entirely, just a small slice); the surgeon says the feeling will come back, but he doesn't say when. Eating is somewhat of a chore. I'm using temporary teeth, and they're not that comfortable, nor are they efficient. It's better than drinking sludge, um, I mean, puréed food, at least mostly, but I can't wait 'til I have solid choppers. The doctor says that it will take a year for the slice in my jaw to completely fill with bone. I hope it's not that long before I can chomp an apple. I'll let you know; I know you're eagerly awaiting the news.

Meanwhile, in case you haven't heard, I'm talking a blue streak. I kind of thought I'd already let you know about that, but some friends are dubious about whether I can talk. Ok, sometimes it's not quite like it was beforehand, but I am talking about as much as I'd like, albeit still sounding a bit like Daffy Duck.

I'm waiting to hear from the radiation doctor about when I start THAT. He asked for a complete medical history, which I was a tad slow in getting to him, and he'll give me an appointment to see him when he gets through that. I had actually thought I'd have heard from him by now, but…

Anyway, that's about all the news that's fit to print… if printing hasn't died out completely by the time you get this. Pray for the continuation of the newspapers and books. Look how well the 78 rpm shellac disc has survived. That should tell you a lot.

Delighted to hear from you if you decide to write (again, in some cases, for the first time in others). I'm really quite warm and fuzzy about my connections with just about all y'all.

Peter

*

Subject: the next installment

Date: Friday, May 22, 2009, 12:04am

Today marks about the first big-item day in the story of my health saga in several weeks. Up 'til now for the past couple of weeks it's just been an incremental getting better, happy-making, but no big whoop, but today I went — at last! — to see the radiation doctor. We spent just about all morning together, going over the details of the radiation. Herewith behold the story thereof.

My first question was: what are the numbers? What percentage of people in my situation have no recurrence with vs. without radiation? Well, it turns out, as per the good Dr L, that there are not nearly enough cases like mine to compile any numbers. That is, adenoid cystic carcinoma is a rare enough cancer in the first place, and, as I think I said before, a very low percentage of those appear on the tongue. In terms of all the ACC's known, the recurrence rate is very high without radiation, and not nearly so high with it. Soo, that just about settles that.

As of right now, pending further input from the technicians, I start on June 8th. That's the Monday after the Manchester gig. Thereafter I go five days a week for the said six or seven weeks. The side effects are a bit hairy at worst. I'm counting on my fabulous constitution to spare me the most extreme effects, but it will probably be a bit tough no matter what. Possible (probable?) side effects include burning both on the outside and inside of the throat area, permanent loss of hair growth on the face (oh, my beautiful beard!), hoarseness and fatigue.

The technical stuff around the radiation is kind of funny. Maybe not funny haha… maybe not funny weird, either. Maybe not funny. Haha. They stuck a big lump of some kind of putty in my mouth to keep my tongue depressed, and wrapped a thermoplastic webbing around my head, all so that when the time comes, they can immobilize my face and keep the radiation as finely aimed as possible. Dr L tells me that the actual radiation time will be no more than about 2-3 minutes per day, but the getting me tacked down, etc., will take up the better part of 15 minutes. Getting to and from the hospital, etc., will take about a half hour each way from my brother's house, 90' from my home, all for a lousy minute or three of actual treatment. Hi ho, hi ho, it's oft berserk we go. Heheheh.

So, that's the story. I have a couple of weeks of grace, and maybe a week or even three of little or no symptoms once I do start, so I'm going to enjoy that time, and maybe even the time afterwards. After all, as I am reminded again and again, it actually beats the alternative by a mile.

Thanks for paying attention. Blessings on you all, believer, atheist, agnostic, and don't-know-what-you-are's.

Peter

*

Subject: news news

Date: Thursday, June 11, 2009, 1:04am

Today was my first day of radiation. That was the *least* of it.

When I walked into the hospital, I was greeted by the good Dr L (may his tribe increase), with the stunning news that about 10 weeks after my surgery, *the cancer is back*.

It's recurred.

I was so taken aback by the news that I wasn't able to ask exactly where and how much, etc. Dr L did say that the chance is still about 80% that they will "get ahead" of the growth, and be able to control, contain, and eventually shrink the tumor.

There's some *more bad news*, however. What I didn't get, if the doctors ever told me, was that ACC (adenoid Cystic Carcinoma) is never considered *completely* cured. This, you may recall, is in direct contradiction to what I was given to understand, or at least what I took to understand. What this means is that, where with some cancers, they test you four times a year, two times a year, once a year, once every five years, then say don't come back. With me, with ACC, it's checking forever. I don't know how often, or any such thing, and while this particular little piece of news is not terribly bleak, it does seem awfully inconvenient.

The radiation treatment I had today (this was Wednesday, at noon) had been re-programmed to accommodate the new diagnosis. I didn't feel a thing. It's a bit intimidating; the big ol' machine is part of a cylinder you're in the center of, and when they turn it, you think you're rotating, until you check your gravity. Beforehand I had what felt like a terra cotta glob stuck in my mouth to keep my tongue depressed. They made a plastic mask to hold my head still, and that got clamped over my face. Not waterboarding, I expect, plus, one keeps reminding oneself that it's all for the good...

The which I do still believe. I will admit to going into shock upon hearing the news; I broke out in a sweat and my hands got all clammy, and my brain was working sufficiently to know that it wasn't working. I've had 12 hours to deal, and I'm beginning to come back to normal, though I'm not rebounding with quite the same elasticity I greeted the original diagnosis with. I guess I'm still pretty optimistic, overall, though, and I look forward to a long time of carrying on with at least nearly my wonted energy and disarray.

Don't anyone get too gushy on me, okay? What I think I need most of all right now is for you-all to remain down-to-earth, clear-minded and unsentimental. Funny stuff is also always appreciated. Easy on the fart jokes, though, right? If not the farts themselves.

Peter

PS. I remain amazed at how many of you there are (six), and I continue to regret that I can't see my way clear to write you each individually. Of course, I'd rather that, if my poor fingers could handle it. Thanks again for your attention and concern.

*

Peter Tork Facebook Page (Official)

19 Sep 2009

Beloved Mob,

I'm pleased to announce I have a clean bill of health. Dr found no indications of any residual tumor(s). I will get a check-up every 3 months, then every 6, then 1x year. ACC can recur, so I'll be getting check-ups for almost the rest of my life, unless I'm 95 and tired, then I might not bother! Short of that, I'll have to be on the *qui vive* henceforth.

Doesn't suck, this clean bill of health thingy.

*

Subject: the state of affairs re: me and my shadow

Date: Tuesday, December 15, 2009 11:08pm

There's good news and, well, just good news on the health front. I just got back from the follow-up visit with Dr. S, who said, and I quote: "You couldn't be better."

This is a clean bill of health — again!, and is, as you might well expect, mightily relieving. It means that there is no evidence of recurrence, and no indication for concern.

I have to go back in four months. This is good news, too; it means that the earlier every-three-month schedule is not necessary. In April I'll go get an x-ray, and we'll go from there. I probably won't send out another one of these 'til then, so, stay well and get better… at whatever you're doing.

I believe that this is not a matter of minimum concern to any of you, and I'm enormously grateful for that.

Thank you all.

Blessings

Peter

*

Peter Tork Facebook Page (Official)

October 11, 2018

A note from Peter regarding some concerns

Dear ones,

there's a lot of stuff going 'round, and I want to let you-all know how it is for me.

While it is true that my health has required a little more attention these days, I'm feeling pretty good. I'm also cherishing this time with family and friends, and making music.

Keep your eyes open for some possible web concerts with friends and other musicians; we'll see what comes down the pipeline.

As for the rest, thanks for your good wishes. This is a private time and I won't be posting updates. Please don't bug the PTFB team either.

So.

Everyone take care of yourselves and your loved ones, and even the occasional random passer-by, eh?

XO, Peter

*

Peter Tork Facebook Page (Official)

FEBRUARY 22, 2019

A Statement from Peter Tork's Family

We are all saddened to share the news that Peter Thorkelson — friend, father, husband, grandfather, philosopher, goofball, entertainer — died peacefully this morning at a family home in Connecticut. Peter succumbed to a 10 year bout with adenoid cystic carcinoma, a rare cancer of the salivary glands. Peter's energy, intelligence, silliness, and curiosity were traits that for decades brought laughter and enjoyment to millions, including those of us closest to him. Those traits also equipped him well to take on cancer, a condition he met with unwavering humor and courage.

We are all still raw, and still have much to process, but we are also feeling appreciation for Peter's contributions. We are grateful that we have an extended support network thanks to the attentive energy and dedication of Peter's fans worldwide. We want those fans to know with absolute certainty that your spirit and goodwill fed Peter with continued energy and force (and of course humor).

With that, we ask that our family have time and space to grieve in privacy.

We are asking fans who would like to make contributions in Peter's name to donate to the scholarship fund at The Institute for The Musical Arts in Massachusetts, a nonprofit that provides young women with music education, music recording, and music community.[48]

Tork About Childhood

I said to my mother once, I held up a teddy bear, and I said, "This bear was damaged in the womb." I don't know where that came from. So following up logically, I asked my mother, I said, "Mother, were you happy to know that you were pregnant with me?"

And she said, "Oh yes, my darling, you don't understand, it meant that I was an adult and my mother couldn't tell me what to do."

My mother didn't get it.

I said, "Oh, I'm so glad I was able to provide you with something!"

I was her little embroidered patch: *Adult*.

I was a ticket, I was a franchise, I was not a person, and I didn't have any way to deal with this. I didn't have any way to sink my teeth into it. This stuff requires *language*. There's no dealing with stuff without language, it's the kind of creature we are, it's the way we're built.[49]

*

We were raised in a middle class, seemingly together home, and no discussion of anything *wrong* was allowed, basically. And the result is that everything that is wrong with the way that I came to, when I grew up and came to life, everything that is wrong with that is compounded by the fact that I have, or had, no way to talk about it.[50]

*

Every time I thought I did something good, my father said, "Don't break your arm patting yourself on the back."[51]

*

My childhood was pleasant. My parents are tickled now about my success, but my younger sister thinks more of me as a Monkee than she does of me as a brother.

I remember a couple of times when my father vented his emotions on me because of circumstances. He didn't mean it the way it sounded to me then. If I had never realized this, it could have left me with a traumatic wound for the rest of my life. Like the time when I was minding my little sister and she went off without my knowing it because I was reading comic books. When he discovered she was missing he yelled at me but later I realized that he did it because he was so worried about her absence. Or the time he shouted, "Be calm!" at me and brought his fist down on the table with such force that I trembled all over. I am told that once — I was too young to remember — I was climbing up on the phonograph and he shouted at me just before the lid of the phonograph struck my head. For many years I couldn't go under anything that had a lid on it without lifting my arm and holding it there to make sure the lid wouldn't fall down.[52]

*

When I was about nine years old, I looked up at the sky and said, "You know, I noticed that when it's cloudy overnight the next day tends to be warmer, like the clouds keep the heat in?"

[My father] turned on me and gave me such a reaction! "What's the matter with you? Do you have a large enough sample to make those conclusions? How can you tell that kind of thing to me!"

All I was doing was saying, "Look what I discovered, Dad." And he wouldn't have it.

So part of my struggle is to create a situation where I get people to pay attention to the things I've discovered. "Look what I found! Look, look, isn't it wonderful?"[53]

*

I did not suffer major physical abuse in my household, I got spanked once or twice when I was small, that's it, not massive abuse by anybody's standards. I was not yelled at, but what did happen for me was that my parents thought I was "okay" as long as I was just a generic kid. As soon as I was who I *really am* they saw that as a *challenge* somehow or other.

My father and I were jogging down the road one day and he said, "Do you want to stop?"

And I said, "No."

He said, "So, you want to race, huh?"

Well that stopped my process.[54]

*

My parents trekked a lot. [Was that a good thing?] No. No, I don't think so. Although it's hard, I've done a fair amount of self examination, for better or for worse, and it might just be that if I'd stayed in one place I'd be just as neurotic as I am today! Maybe my parents drove me to it? Maybe if I'd stayed in one place I'd have been a trombone teacher or something, at some point, at some place.[55]

*

My life between then [moving to Connecticut] and my senior year of high school was a total disaster. In fifth grade I started going downhill because I was unhappy. I was constantly trying to make friends and trying to be funny but never succeeding because I was so much younger. I did have a small circle of friends but that was at home, it didn't have much to do with school.[56]

*

All of my early life was spent feeling out of whack. Physically, I matured late and never was very athletic and always found myself on the short end of the stick. I was raised in a liberal family in the middle of the McCarthy era.[57]

*

From [first grade], until I got to college, I was always about a year younger than the other kids. A year makes a hell of a difference in school. Kids don't like getting involved with someone they consider to be their junior. It didn't make things too easy.[58]

*

I remember when I was thirteen, I put a loaded gun to my head. Loaded and cocked. I eventually put it down. And a couple of days later I sort of realized — or decided — that I preferred to live. Part of it was that I really wanted them to *get* how angry and distressed I was, but I also wanted to be around to watch [my parents] go through the changes. And I realized I couldn't do both. So I had to let the "I'll show them" side of it go.[59]

*

A conversation with James Lee Stanley during their first Two Man Band road trip

Peter:

Do you know, my father didn't even *ask* me if I wanted to move to Connecticut!

James:

Well, weren't you *eight* years old?

Peter:

Yes…

James:

Well, I don't think I would ask my eight year old son if I could take a job in Connecticut, I think I would just move. I don't think he was *disregarding* you.

Days later on the return drive home after having stayed at Peter's parents' home in Connecticut

James:

Listen, did you ever talk to your father about *why* he moved? Because *I* did.

I asked him, "Listen, how come you moved from Wisconsin to Connecticut? All the relatives were also in Wisconsin so you moved *away* from the family thing that supported Peter. Why did you do that?"

And he said, "Well, to tell you truth, James, I got offered a job down at the southern end of Illinois, and I got offered the job in Connecticut at the University. I thought: *No, we should be closer to the family.* So I drove down to the Illinois-Kentucky border and I checked into that job, which was a good paying job, everything was nice… *except…* the place had *white and colored* water fountains, and *white and colored* bathrooms, and *white and colored* restaurants. I didn't want to expose my children to that kind of bigotry, so I took the *other* job."

Peter:

Nah… Nah…

Peter grows quiet, and then gets choked up

Peter:

Thank you.[60]

Tork About Community-ism

I have a transcendent belief in the people (in the long run, that is, knowing that individuals are all flawed). I believe there are certain things which are true across all of humanity, though I don't know what they all are. I probably don't know what 1% of them are, but I'm sure they're there! I believe that community is built into us (we are social animals, after all.)[61]

*

There's this Latin expression and it means, the thing speaks for itself. The song ["A Better World"] said to me what I've already known all along but have never been able to express in such a pithy way, succinctly: *there's more than enough.*

The subtext is that what's keeping us from all having enough is *fear*. And politics, which is fear. And there is no way to eliminate fear from the human experience, but there are ways to allay that fear to an appreciable extent. And if we know there's enough, that makes things a little calmer, makes things a little less grabby.

Because in the material world, in a zero sum game, if there's only so much food to go around, if I take too much, you don't have enough. But if I take enough, you have enough too. And that will happen if we are not terrified of each other and the vagaries of life, which you can't stop, life goes on. It's weird, people get hit by cars, get brought down by cancer or some other disease, or trip and fall and hit their heads, this kind of thing happens all the time and there's no stopping it. But the more fear we bring to the situation, the tougher it is on everybody. The fearful and the feared as well.[62]

*

A lot of what was true then about me, is true now. I'm still boundlessly optimistic, I just had to revise my time scale is all. I thought things were going to come together in a matter of decades, now I think it's going to take a couple of centuries, if not millennia.

I see it as an evolutionary necessity — as part of the human race (to get serious for a while) the system of interplay in this country, and over the vast majority of the surface of the world, which values competition, individualism, and essentially aggression, over the forces of co-operativism and community as a system, which is inherently damaging to each and every one of us, and evolutionarily necessary — to abandon the sucker and get on with the business of getting together. Because, as I once said in a reasonably spontaneous mode, we have to stick together or we're all going to come unglued together.

Capitalism is on the way down! Socialism and communism is the only conceivable way that we're going to get — no don't use those words! Community-ism! Co-operativism! Basically capitalism fosters aggressiveness.

Now here is the situation. In so far as there is just enough to go around, every time somebody has got more than he needs, somebody else has less than they need and is dying of starvation and lack of material well-being.

In so far as there is more than enough to go around, maybe there's a little room for some people to play around with, however, until we get everybody to the level of "they all have what they need" and we're secure at least on that material basis, we won't *know* if there's enough to go around, or not.[63]

*

The vast majority of people in the country today believe themselves to be inherently, deeply, uniquely, and rarely *flawed*. Everybody thinks that they, unlike everybody else, are badly broken and out of whack in some kind of way… and to the contrary… each and every one of them was a perfectly viable human being, perfectly ready to go out and be people!

The therapeutic coalescing is the bringing together of your own capacity for objective analysis and support. The child in you is, of course, insecure and dependent, and the adult in you is, of course, independent and secure and aware, but people in a schizophrenia — which incidentally means "broken-heartedness" as well as "broken-mindedness", if you go back to the greek roots — so in their schizophrenic situation their adult and their child don't relate very well, they do not stroke themselves in real ways, because they've been told they're not *allowed* to. "You don't get to say that you're all right!" We as a culture tend to remove ourselves from our own support systems, and this happens inter-personally as well as intra-personally, (I don't do that as well by myself, and I do not support people except in rare circumstances, as we are beginning to come together, as in therapy.)

Now, most of us feel that we are uniquely, deeply, and specially flawed, unlike anybody else. And this is a lie, which has been foisted on us by those people who would like to keep us separate in order to keep us working against each other. Because as long as we keep ourselves separate, and as long as we go on the basis that one person's gain is another person's loss, we are going to go on on a basis where we will regard that as true in the national economy too. But the converse is truer. That is, as we shift over to a co-operative, where working together is the main emphasis, and individual effort is the lesser emphasis, we will all gain much more rapidly, and that is why I promote the community-ist and co-operativist systems, as opposed to capitalist.

End of speech![64]

Tork About Davy Jones

One kid did get special treatment. Davy Jones walked through [the auditioning process] like he owned the place. But I've grown to love him now. I do.[65]

*

Micky's the best pal, but my heart connection is biggest with Davy. Davy is capable of as much heart as anyone I've ever met. I kind of had a crush on Davy for a while.[66]

*

I like, respect and love each of the guys in different proportions. Somehow or other, though, Jonesy got my heart. I don't know why, because I don't like him very much. Sometimes he's great to hang with and sometimes he's very difficult, which is not so true of the other two.[67]

*

Davy in his most sensitive and aware moments was a true gem. And of all of those guys, it is *Davy* whom I have any sense of real affection for, and love. I do love the man.

There were times when he could be an absolute unmentionable, in fact unfortunately that was the majority of the time, but still, when he was *on*, when he was *open* and when he was *sensitive*, he was amazingly open and sensitive and I've heard him lay off remarks just out of the corner of his mouth, only meant for me to hear that just revealed such depths of feeling and emotion that I was absolutely staggered, and I've been staggered on a number of occasions by the man.

Also, there was the time that he staggered me with a left hook. That was a little more difficult to put up with.[68]

*

We were getting on each other's nerves, and suddenly Davy was shouting and cursing everybody in general and whoever was in the line of fire, specifically. I went over to try to calm him down.

"Get out of here, you twit!" he screams.

I didn't move, and the next thing I know, he hits me in the mouth with his forehead — a nutter, as the English call it. Pretty lethal.

So, we started at each other — arms flailing. The crew broke us up. We were held off each other by about three men apiece — still glaring, and struggling to get loose. Finally, we calmed down.

"Okay, Peter?"

"Okay."

"Okay, Davy?"

"Okay."

But we're good actors, remember? As they loosened their grip, I got free first and slugged him as hard as I could.

I was surprised. It felt good.[69]

*

First and only time I ever hit anybody, besides my brother, in anger. I socked Davy and it took two stitches to close him.

I came around afterwards, we went to the infirmary, Ward [Sylvester] and I (Ward was Davy's manager before this whole thing started up). We went to the infirmary, and we were gonna look in on him, and I called in.

I said, "Davy, are you there?"

"What do you want?"

"I just wanna see if you're all right."

He said, "Get outa here before I flatten you."

And Ward and I grinned and walked away, 'cos what Davy was saying was, "It's all right". But you wouldn't have known, I mean, you just had to know him to know that it *was* all right. And then he just didn't say anything else to me. As far as that was concerned, that's the last that incident was ever mentioned. And Davy was perfectly cheerful and friendly to me from then on.

He had it coming to him, the little son-of-a-bitch should not have tried to sock me with his head that way. He was really acting like a punk and he deserved it, and he knew it. And he felt good about it. At least as far as I was concerned, he seemed to accept it.[70]

*

You *do* start having rows. But the stories about us, put around in some papers… not true. It's just that I find Davy too tall and that irritates me![71]

*

We were filming interviews for the show. They said, "Let's roll." Davy got down on the floor and rolled. I looked at this kid and thought, I've never seen anybody do anything nonsensical like that. I mean I was a goofy kid in a lot of ways, but only when I was confident. And here were these guys, perfectly confident. The cameras were rolling. I was nervous as heck. And these guys were doing goofy things like that. I learned a lot from them.[72]

*

It is with great sadness that I reflect on the sudden passing of my long-time friend and fellow-adventurer, David Jones. His talent will be much missed; his gifts will be with us always.

My deepest sympathy to Jessica and the rest of his family.

Adios, to the Manchester Cowboy.[73]

*

We dearly miss our dear departed brother; our brother in arms; the small one, now what's his name, it will come to me in a minute. We called him the Manchester Cowboy. Davy had a love affair; a brief flirtation with country music for a little while and we called him the Manchester Cowboy from that, and it stuck. It's all fond memories.[74]

*

He's very gracious that way [staying after a show until each and every autograph was signed]. He was a master in many aspects of this kind of thing. We had some very wonderful personal connections and I'm really sad to see all that gone.[75]

*

What stood out for me with Davy as an artist was his spontaneous stagecraft. He enjoyed himself on stage, for sure, gloried in his part. He was so alert as an entertainer and so relaxed that things would come to him out of the blue and he would just go with them. He could be incredibly funny. Micky and I were always breaking up on stage. I'm so sorry he's gone. I'm going to miss that wit and heart.[76]

*

The end of the last tour [was the last contact I had with Davy — July 23, 2011]. We just said, "Goodbye, I'll see you soon." I didn't think I *wouldn't* – partly because he was the youngest of us. That was too bad.[77]

*

I wrote an article after the death of Michael Jackson in which I meditated upon the inner life of the pop star. Now comes the loss of my sometime partner, Davy Jones, and I'm in an entirely different position. I was close to David (as I almost always called him), and I got to know him as few others could. I've often said I loved, liked and respected each of the other three Monkees in different proportions. What I don't often say is that I loved David the most.

When we first met, I was confronted with a slick, accomplished, young performer, vastly more experienced than I in the ways of show biz, and yes, I was intimidated. Englishness was at a high premium in my world, and his experience dwarfed my entertainer's life as a hippie, basket-passing folk singer on the Greenwich Village coffee house circuit. If anything, I suppose I was selected for the cast of "The Monkees" TV show partly as a rough-hewn counterpart to David's sophistication.

What stands out for me about David, however, were the several events through the years in which I came to see a man of extraordinary heart and sympathy. First comes first:

We had just been selected as co-cast members and introduced to each other. Shake hands, "How do you do?"

The producers sent us out to the desert, a drive of a couple of hours, to film a commercial for Kellogg's, which was sponsoring the show. We were almost entirely silent throughout the drive.

"Nice day."

"Huh."

Silence.

"Anyone hungry?"

"Hunh."

We pulled into a diner, sat down and ordered.

For some reason, Micky Dolenz's and my salads came first. He and I basically stuck our forks into the bowls, and put whatever came up into our mouths.

"You pigs!" David said. "Anyone would think you was raised in a bahn the ways you guys is eatin'!"

Micky and I were shamefaced.

David's salad came. With all eyes upon him, he carefully cut the salad into one-inch strips, turned the bowl 90 degrees and cut the strips into one-inch squares. He doused it all with creamy dressing. Then, he reached into the bowl, grabbed a fistful of the salad and smashed it into his face.

I suppose he felt he'd overdone the manners maven thing and was making it up to us, but it was the style and willingness to go overboard that was so appealing, and more to the point, so very funny.

I laugh to this day thinking about it.

The Monkees (the group now, not the TV series) took a lot of flack for being "manufactured," by which our critics meant that we hadn't grown up together, paying our dues, sleeping five to a room, trying to make it as had the Beatles and Rolling Stones.

Furthermore, critics said, The Monkees first albums (remember albums?) were almost entirely recorded by professional studio musicians, with hardly any input from any of us beyond lead vocals.

I felt this criticism keenly, coming as I did from the world of the ethical folk singer, basically honoring the standards of the naysayers.

We *did* play as a group live on tour, including a concert in Osaka, Japan, in 1968. There, in the middle of a performance of Mike Nesmith's "Sunny Girlfriend," we hit the pocket. The beat fell into place, solid and grooving. Rock 'n' roll was happening there for us on stage.

David came bouncing over to me and yelled above the volume, "WE'RE GONNA FORM A GROUP!"

David's sympathy for my feelings about the criticism, his musical awareness and his sense of humor buoyed me that day about as much as getting into the groove.

Later, when we four argued to be the musicians on our own albums, it was David's agreement that provided the unanimity that made the difference. This was *huge*, actually; Micky and David came from an entirely different tradition. Actors sang on records made for them, and nobody thought twice about it. Folkies and rockers made their own albums!

There were many such incidents, but I hope these help to convey David Jones' sympathy, humor and heart, qualities always in too short supply.

He's yukkin' it up somewhere else, now.[78]

*

The man was unique and a huge, huge talent. We're not going to replace him. [Davy] was such a little heartthrob. I don't think people knew how bright and talented and gifted he was in all things. I've come to believe he was, in his own way, the smartest, most musically talented and best actor among us.[79]

*

In the outpouring of grief over Davy's death (my grief, and the grief in the community), I have been reminded of many things that were unique about our shared experience in *The Monkees* TV show, as well as our subsequent reunions and dis-unions.

Regarding Davy's death, I hoped to touch upon more deeply the richness of our relationship, which covered parts of six decades. A presence, and an absence now, that defies definition. I have yet to find the right words. Perhaps there simply are none, but I want to note that when I said I liked, loved and respected each bandmate in different ratios, it was Davy that I loved most.[80]

*

Who I miss is Davy of course. Davy is the guy who… I've always said I loved, liked and respected [the band members] in different proportions, but Davy actually kinda got my heart.[81]

*

I only now have, in the last couple of years, come to understand how smart and good-hearted Davy Jones could be. I did not have the skills to notice that, even though I was drawn to it without knowing exactly why. But I certainly did not have the first clue of how to encourage all of the good stuff from Davy that I loved. I wish I could have known how to do it — and he might still be with us, even.[82]

*

Thank you for the opportunity to contribute some memories at this memorial for David Thomas Jones, Davy to you.

I am truly at a loss for words, mostly remembering moments that pale in the telling of them. I carry so many images of Davy through the years: the bright teen at the center of The Monkees TV show, the witty prankster, always with a joke (not always a *new* joke, but always a joke!), the dedicated horseman, the devoted family man, and the gifted performer who captured hearts around the world. Davy adored performing, and adored meeting and greeting his fans. He was tireless in making himself available to sing a song, do a dance, shake a hand; whatever was asked.

I had heart-to-heart moments with him that were among the best in my life. I was blessed to know and work closely with him. He was one in about six billion, give or take. We won't see his like again. He left much too soon. I share your sadness. Thank you again for this chance to contribute. God bless and keep you all.[83]

Tork About Death

As to my understanding of what happens when I (or you) die, I base my understanding on something I believe to be true, which is that, however much we may talk about things in their parts, they are not actually parts making up a whole, but rather partial ways of seeing. The buddha said (I am told) that you can separate the flame from the fire, but only in your mind. Therefore, I believe that when the person dies, it all stops. I don't believe that there is a part of our individual selves which is not subject to the laws of decay. Meanwhile, I do take heart from the parallel notion that just as the body decays and becomes part of new life, so, too, our understanding and ideals become part of some new combination of thought yet to come.

But as to my individual self continuing past death and re-emerging in another incarnation, or in some real estate in the sky relieved of all trouble, no. (Heaven is in your mind, as the old Traffic song said.)[84]

*

It seems to me that some spirits don't believe they can go anywhere, or they just feel a need to hang around after their bodies have split. It all depends on your own individual spirit whether you go or stay.[85]

*

A good attitude generates more comfort. When people say, "Why me?" and "How could this happen?" or "Somebody must be made to pay for my problems," that attitude is a low-skill approach. It's not very contentment-making.

I don't like pain and I don't want to hurt, but the sheer fact of dying in and of itself is of no consequence to me. When I die, there won't be a "me" of any kind. There won't be anything, no collection of what we think of as an immutable, individual something or other.[86]

Tork About Despair

The lowest depth of despair is the conviction that I'm all alone, that there is no help. There's no help and no hope. Boy, that just about put me away when I was thirteen.[87]

*

I saw myself as the victim of forces, the product not of myself, but of other people, places, and things. I was in therapy for about a year when I was a teenager, and I learned that whatever happens to me in life is a function of my own choices – but I lost sight of that for a long time.[88]

*

The saddest day of my life? Probably the day my cat got run over when I was about nine. I haven't been close to a pet since.[89]

*

Any twelve-step disease — alcoholism, compulsive over-eating, sexoholism, shopping, compulsive relationships — any of those things, they all serve the same purpose, in my view. All of these diseases, if you want to call them that, "negative syndromes", have in common that the behavior is about shutting out the part of your life that tells you what a rotten person you are.

Me! Rotten person.

I heard: *It must be your fault that you don't have any friends; there is something wrong with you.*

There *was* something wrong with me. But I didn't have any idea what it was, so I thought there was something wrong with me. I thought that there was a basic character, deep-seated evil seed in me someplace that could not be rooted out, and I was doomed to live with it the rest of my life.

And it took me down, and it killed me, and I was helpless before it. That's what I thought. And drinking shut that information out.

And I think I see it in other people. That their behaviors shut that voice out. Unfortunately that's the same set of brain cells that enables you to get in touch with any kind of a spirituality either, so as long as I was drinking I couldn't get in touch with a dependability, a higher power.

So, fortunately, somewhere along the line, the information came through to me, there was no more hope of pretense. I was drinking. I knew I was in trouble. I wanted to quit. I couldn't quit. I didn't know that I couldn't drink at all, safely. I thought, if I could find a way to drink just a little bit I'd be all right. And in fact, I'm sure of that to this day! But I'm also sure that I can *not* drink just a little bit. And I finally got it, that I had no such option.[90]

*

There's a very good chance that if you can abstain from the chemistry, your depression will eventually lighten up. This applies to anxiety, too. If it doesn't, then at least you'll be in a much better position to know which is doing what.

Meanwhile don't do anything radical and/or hasty, which could prove to be a permanent solution to a temporary problem. There is no situation so dire that it can't be remedied, or improved, or at the very least faced with calm. This takes time, practice and help, but these are all available to you in the recovery rooms, and while the chances that you'll face abuse there is not zero, it is certainly very low.[91]

*

I'm amazed at people's inability to accept help, sometimes, but I know I felt much easier being *of help* than I did *accepting* it. (I imagine it's part of the self-denigrating pressure of authoritarian society.)[92]

*

There is most certainly no time limit on grieving. I do believe there is a psychological limit, though. I don't know how exactly to put this, but (for starters), I am sure that if there is no let-up in the sadness, then there are unmet issues waiting to be dealt with. In other words, it's not the grief that matters but rather the underlying belief that some irreplaceable chance has been lost. Loss of a parent is always tough, but it's the least unnatural order of things, if you see what I'm saying. Perhaps you might check out some bereavement groups to hear how others are dealing with the same thing.

Still and all, it is actually not true that the loss of a parent is the loss of an irreplaceable chance. Whatever you feel you lost can be reclaimed in your life. It's not easy, as I can attest, but it can be done. Always and always I turn to community. I have found my greatest strength and growth, spiritual and psychological, from my communities and the members thereof. Stick with people who are on your side without ulterior motive, and you can't go too far wrong.

There's much more that this kicks up for me that I can't get into for space limitations, so I'm sorry if I can't be much more help in this forum. But I can promise that your situation is not remotely hopeless.

As to those who are giving you grief about your grief, well, basically, and not to put too fine a point on it, fuck 'em if they can't take a joke.[93]

*

I've grown not to believe in tragedy. I've grown to believe that all things work out for the best. Even if you're in despair, you're going to discover that there's more will to live in you than all your despair, and you'll come out of it. The will to live is a will to be cheerful, and to be on top of things. Stay cheerful![94]

*

I lost a good friend to despair, I'm sure it was to despair. A man named Jerry Renino was *The Monkees*' bass player. We had a backup band, and he was our main man. He did himself in, and I'm convinced it was because he couldn't relinquish his role as the Go-To guy, he was The Man. He couldn't relinquish that role, and ultimately, I think he couldn't ask for help.

They say in real estate, there's only three issues: location, location, location. In life, there's only three things to remember: *get help, get help, get help*.[95]

*

You ARE worthy of love. Ask whatever you've got for a power greater than yourself (you know, God, or the sense of the universe, whatever) for help in the morning, and say thanks for paying attention at the end of the day.

If you do not have a higher power, make up one who loves you regardless.[96]

Tork About Despair

Tork About Education

I was raised in the formalist tradition. I was taught to speak well in the womb.[97]

*

I grew up with this tremendous vocabulary, and I don't seem able to shake it off. I wish I could. It would speed up conversation![98]

*

Intimidate people? Yeah I'm afraid I do sometimes. I don't mean to, particularly, but part of it is from that insecurity. Part of the reason people build up these skills at, say intellectualization, is out of insecurity. And I was raised thinking, with the tenet of: perfection is barely tolerable. If you're not perfect, it's intolerable. And that same insecurity will build up into, "Boom! Here's my vast intellectual storehouse, chump!" So people will get intimidated, but obviously that's not my point, I have no innate desire to blow people away. I get a lot more understanding laughing with people; that's basically my feedbag.[99]

*

I flunked out of college. Twice. Same school. You'd think one of us would have gotten the hint, right?[100]

*

The only school is Life itself. I flunked out from school because I didn't care. I couldn't stand the way education was being given in my school, or any other school. I wanted desperately to learn, but I was too interested and I kept drifting off into daydreams. Some of the teachers understood, but they couldn't save me from being thrown out. Grades are the thing. Education is being made as dull as a cold fish.

What we need are imaginative schools like your Summer Hill, where kids can learn whatever they want to, and have some choice in the pace they will set. Education needs to live, not come out of stuffy books.[101]

*

I was out doing dance dates with bands and I knew I had something inside me wanting to get out, and that it was to do with music. I eventually had to level with myself and admit that I just didn't care enough about mere scholastic ability. I wanted more.[102]

*

Well, [why did I decide to go to school in Minnesota, at Carleton?] It was — it was *easy*. It's my father's alma mater. And therefore they took me. (laughs)

I had this unfortunate situation of having lots and lots of potential and very little actualization, as it were. You know, the great SAT scores and not great grades. But I think, you know, they weighted children of alumni so much, so heavily, that they took me. They would've probably taken me if I'd been psychotic.

I didn't think I had any problem concentrating on academia, my problem was that I didn't do enough of it. (laughs) Actually, what happened was, I really was so deeply involved in all the extracurricular activities. I was in the orchestra, I played French horn for year, it was wonderful. And I was in theater. And I was a DJ on KARL radio.

It's a funny thing. I wouldn't say [the priorities were a little mixed up], I would say my priorities were in perfect order. Carleton did not agree, of course. I should say, they agreed, but the priorities were not their priorities for the students. Because as it turns out, obviously my priorities were in perfect order. I was into music and broadcasting and showbiz, which is where I belonged, and always did as it turns, but I didn't know that at the time. See, that's the thing about it. Having flunked out of Carleton College, I mean, that's probably one of the better things that happened to me in my career. I have them to thank for that.

A couple years ago, a few Carleton students held a portrait of the former Carleton president hostage until the school named a pinball room after you. What do you think of that?

I actually have rarely been so graced with an honor. As a matter of fact, I think I can truly say it is one of the singular highest honors I've ever received. When I heard about the news, I practically collapsed in gratitude.

I went [back to visit] this past — not this past summer, summer before this past — it brought a wave of nostalgia. It's interesting because the nostalgia that I had was for a time I never really partook in. The groves of Academe, you know… suddenly seemed very, very attractive to me because it's the cloistering, the ability, the chance to delve into whatever it is that you're doing without obstruction, without distraction. That looked awfully attractive to me at the time, and I felt it too, but I don't know that that's ever to be.[103]

*

One of the worst things about [getting a degree], I know, is having to put up with this chore for a few years while waiting for a pretty good payoff.

You are in a situation where you may suffer serious setbacks if you can't hang in there, and it doesn't sound like you have much support anyplace. (Parents no good for you in this? Parents often don't get it, I know, particularly at your age. They seem to have universally developed a blind spot about kids in your age group. A nasty phenomenon, for sure.)[104]

*

Look at it this way, schools — public, private and colleges — are strictly vocational institutions. Yeah, you got to have degrees if you want to get somewhere. If you want to *think*, you do that someplace else. There is no compulsion for schools to teach knowledge. They do not teach wisdom. They do not teach people how to think.[105]

*

In life, experience is the only teacher.

I mean, you don't really know how it is to fall in love just by reading a book about it.[106]

*

Sometimes I think I would like to teach, but not in a college bound by the ordinary compartmentalized divisions. I would teach humanity, and you would have to incorporate things like anthropology and philosophy into that, and it would have to be the kind of school where I could teach without a degree. I don't think I would go back for one.[107]

*

After Marin County I went to Southern California and sort of assembled a family. My daughter from my previous marriage came to live with me and my woman, who I then married and had a son with. Then I taught school. There I was, a married father of two, and a nice square career teaching school.

Well, it was the best offer I had. (Spoken in hippie drawl) *Hey, man, I just go where the four winds blow, man.* I taught for a year and a half, then the organization collapsed. It was called Pacific Hills School in Santa Monica and it was gorgeous. I was teaching English, social studies, tutoring a little bit of math, science, phys. ed and music. I had a rock band class — there was one guy whose fingers just flew. I had one woman who played flute in the rock band and with her on cello and me on guitar we did a Bach piece together; it was splendid.[108]

*

I was a schoolteacher in Southern California, and I taught music as well as academics, and I really very much love to teach, and, and I think that if circumstances show me that I am not to entertain anymore or my entertaining career per se winds down, I would very, very much love to coach young entertainers.[109]

*

As a teacher, I realized that in order to teach something well you need to understand what your student is going through as they try to learn.[110]

*

I was a very unfunny kid in school. One of these wise-ass loudmouths who keeps trying to say funny things but can't. They're awful. You know how awful that type is. I was that type. I had somebody like that when I was teaching school last year — he's not at the school this year, bless his heart. He was impossible to take. I told him once that as crazy as he was, not to forget: Look what happened to me![111]

*

When you ask me if I'm doing anything important between then and now, I hear you asking me: have I done anything that has been noticed particularly by any large body of people? The answer is no, I haven't had a large influence, I haven't made a loud noise, and I haven't done anything that has reached a lot of people in a lot of ways.

I taught school for three years, and to me, that was pretty important because I was dealing, you know, at the closest level possible on one-to-one. But that's not going to get me my fame and fortune. It's important, but it's not loud.

Memorable? Yes, but memorable by whom? I think some of my former students are gonna remember that I was their teacher for a while. That was all right. You have to remember that, in this society, teaching is not regarded as a very important pastime by those people in charge of setting budgets and national priorities and that kind of thing. Because if it were, they'd be paid a vastly greater amount of money than they are. Not, you know, double doesn't begin to get it. Triple, quadruple, that kind of thing maybe. And the fact that teachers are paid as poorly as they are indicates what the priorities are. Nurses make what garbage men make, that kind of thing. It speaks… well… ill, it speaks very poorly, and very loudly about our priorities. That's not my business in the large sense, all I can do is play the games as they are laid out before me. And having some modest influence in the style with which I play them. That seems to be about it.[112]

*

I prefer something a bit serious, so I can baffle people with my massive intellect.[113]

Tork About Facing Morbidity

Late last year, after a few months of my not swallowing in a normal way, a friend mentioned that my voice sounded funny, kind of squawky and nasal. I'd meant to get it checked out, but her observation pushed me to doing something about it sooner rather than later. I went to an ear, nose and throat doctor, who sprayed my nostrils with anesthetic and sent a length of fiber-optic cable up my nose and down my throat. He came back with bad news. There was a growth on the lower region of my tongue. He suspected squamous cell carcinoma.

I don't count myself as being afraid to die, but the news hit me like a fist to the chest.

A subsequent biopsy and pathology exam showed that I had adenoid cystic carcinoma.

Adenoid cystic carcinoma, ACC to the cognoscenti, is a relatively rare cancer, usually occurring in the salivary glands. Mine occurred on the lower part of my tongue; that's even rarer. I wound up in New York at Memorial Sloan-Kettering Cancer Center, where one Dr. Jatin Shah told me I should get surgery as soon as possible. I thought about it a second and said I wasn't doing anything that afternoon…

Dr. Shah laughed and amended: as soon as practicable. That turned out to be the following Wednesday. I woke up from that surgery with another tube up my nose and down my throat — this one for feeding me. About three months later I began a follow-up course of radiation at a high-tech hospital in Boston, where they rev up a cyclotron and pipe protons down the hall and through a giant metal tube into my throat. (Remember electrons, neutrons and protons? Those.)

My friend, Therra Gwyn, who is also my editor and publicist, suggested that if the news of my cancer seeped out without my having a say in it, it would most likely get so distorted that there'd be 30 stories out there, none of them with more than a tangential relationship with the actuality. Better she said — and I agreed — to tell the story myself, as best I could. Besides making sure the record was straight, telling the story out loud on a Web site and Facebook page might help the world (or that part of it that was interested) relax some fears about cancer in general and might boost attention to adenoid cystic carcinoma in particular. Also, it might just help me keep a right-sized attitude about life and myself. Otherwise, you know, it'd be like: I'm a celebrity, get me offa this planet! Can't have that.

As of this writing, I'm just beginning to feel the effects of the second course of radiation, a bit of soreness on the tongue, some unpleasant effects when swallowing. So far, not too bad.

I have a couple of performance dates lined up, which I've opted not to cancel. I know I'm taking a chance here, because one of the side effects of the radiation is supposed to be hoarseness. The radiologist told me, "Well, you play guitar and you sing. Perhaps you won't sing, but maybe you'll play guitar a lot more."

I recovered very quickly after my surgery, and I've been hoping that my better-than-average constitution will keep the worst effects of radiation at bay. My voice and energy still seem to be in decent shape, so maybe I can pull these gigs off after all. Just in case, though, I've invited some friends to join me, including my friend Lauren, a world-class slide guitar player. People will be so dazzled by her that they won't notice whether I'm doing well. I'm also bringing in belly dancers, and I'm expecting a fly-over by the Royal Canadian Air Force. Maybe elephants.

I mean to do those shows.[114]

*

I couldn't swallow and food seemed to stick in my throat. I had to chew more than usual. But it didn't bother me much and otherwise I felt fine.

However, a few months later, a friend said: "Hey, Peter, your voice is sounding funny — you should get it checked out."

The tumour [which was the size of a plum] went right from my tongue down my throat. It was a major procedure. They cut all the way down from my lower lip into my throat and opened my jaw bone to get to the part of the neck and throat where the tumour was located.

The cancer has also done a number on my salivary glands. I often have a dry mouth. That's permanent. I sometimes have a bit of trouble hitting the upper mid-range notes — but I think I'm singing better than ever.[115]

*

Did I change my philosophy after I got my diagnosis? No, I have to say I didn't. I've been at this business of figuring out my life for a long time, and if I didn't have a philosophy of life that included the possibility of having cancer, and even of dying of it, well, then I haven't done a good job in crafting a working philosophy, have I?

If, on the other hand, you mean: Did I discover how quickly and well I bounce back from radiation treatment? Well, yeah, I'm a lucky guy, and I learned that to a new extent during the course of this adventure.

When I got my initial diagnosis, I admit I had a good cry for a bit. Crying wasn't part of my plan, exactly, but neither was it a black mark in my book, as far as I'm concerned.

The gift was that immediately afterwards, I was able to ask what the next thing was to do, and went about *doing* that without a lot of "Why me?" or other such attitudes I regard as diversionary.

I highly recommend keeping the question, "What's the next right thing?" at the forefront of the mind as an antidote to self-pity and other distractions. It works for me.[116]

*

My perspective on life hasn't changed a bit as a result of having (had) cancer. I've worked kind of hard on my attitude toward life, and damn cheap it would have been, too, if I hadn't made provision in it for illness and death, wouldn't it?[117]

*

Well, folks, I truly am a very lucky man to be able to keep playing the music I love through all these years and changes, and I have you all to thank for that. Thank you!

In addition to offering my thanks, I feel moved to remind you all to take care of yourselves, and get check-ups. To that point: this year I am participating in a health campaign to encourage early detection of head and neck cancers, with free screenings offered around the country on the week of April 22-28.

I am grateful that in March 2009 my cancer was detected early enough for me to undergo successful surgery and follow-up treatment. Please take advantage of these free screenings. Early detection and treatment can improve outcomes, so get screened and increase your chances for living a full and healthy life.[118]

Tork About Forgiveness

Fear. As far as I'm concerned, that's the only reason for not acting honorably and forthrightly. Time has a way of healing wounds. Wounding heels, too, come to that.

Meanwhile, might I suggest that you check out the exact nature of your decisions…? Believe me, I am absolutely not suggesting that you compromise your principles and agree to kowtow, only that you check out your emotions for unhealthy sentiments like revenge and self-pity. Those will mess you up worse. The idea is to forgive to the best of your ability, which only means that you get that [they] behaved as well as [they] could, however poorly that was. It certainly does NOT mean to cave. Get it? Forgive them and leave them alone; they're not a happy camper, however much they think they made the right choice. No happy person treats somebody the way you tell me they've treated you.

I'm sad for your situation; it's pretty awful. The only consolation I can offer you is that you probably will develop into a deeply caring person, and you will (maybe partly) thank this situation — strange as it may sound — for your growing empathy and good-heartedness. I wish this for you. I hope for good cheer for you in spite of all.[119]

*

I'm no authority on Buddhism. Nor Christianity, for that matter. But my understanding of Jesus' message is that forgiveness — understanding that the next person is a fellow struggler in his/her path, just like me, and that none of us can judge the next one — is critical to our well-being. Personally I believe that that message, whether you're a Christian or not, is an absolutely necessary understanding for keeping the planet from going up in atomic vaporization, or dying of heat stroke and carbon dioxide poisoning.

What I understand the Buddha to have indicated includes the realization that all things are a living, pulsing part of this world, rocks and rockers both. That tells me that my job is to fit into this world with the least disruption possible.

I guess that Buddhism isn't as specific on the question as Christianity is, but I believe that implicit in the two philosophies is the understanding that to *not* forgive is to make my own life the more difficult, never mind how much more trouble I cause in the outside world if I think I have a right to seek vengeance, or even to harbor a grudge.

I hope that's useful.

Tork About Freedom

It is said, in a certain school of esoterica, that when you first get the hint of it, the mountains are no longer the mountains and the moon is no longer the moon. But when you get past it and come out the other side, with some journeyman mastery, shall we say, the mountains are all mountains again, and the moon is a moon.

I think I'm at that stage with my life. When I first got the awareness of the extramundane, things just became all holy and completely beyond rational understanding. It was the first flush of acid, the first social explosion of the hippie era. "Everything is everything" and "Wonderfulness is wonderfulness" absolutely swamped the factual reality of a chair. Chairs were no longer chairs; they were imbued with mystery and magic. Having lived with that and taken a few hard knocks on the basis of overdoing it, I've entered what I call the tertiary stage of things.

The first stage is where things are what they are. You've got goals and dreams and hopes, but there's no magic. Then you find the magic and it's *all* magic and nothing is real. Now there is reality *and* there is magic; they're *both* real.

It's what I call the Church of Three. You have a starting point that's essentially unitary. Then comes the binary, the secondary phase, where everything is broken up and shattered and shot into millions of pieces. From there, you must have a dialectic. The third stage must appreciate and understand and value the first without undercutting and devaluing the second. It's no good just to talk about the positive. If the negative is there, you can't shut it out. For a while there wasn't any negative. Then it came into our lives in real ways, in ways we had to come to grips with. So, there we were, in the middle of stage two, shattered and broken, not believing in stage one anymore. Then comes stage three. This is where we recognize that there are times to slip into that primary mode and times when it won't do. If you insist on sticking to that mode, you're going to get your nose broken. And that's what happened.

So there comes a time when, in full awareness of stage one, you behave through stage two, to get your stage three – a transcendent involvement of both stages.[120]

*

The burden of "operating your life" is the anchor in everybody's life — the drag in everybody's life — at all times. If you can dispense with it, you are free. I call that the third state.

Where the first state is, you don't care because you're a baby and everybody takes care of everything.

Then there's the middle state, where you have to mind the rules.

And if you ever get away from having to mind the rules, that's the third. The burden of monitoring your life is lifted.[121]

Tork About Happiness

The question of happiness is such a big one that I'm not sure I can do more than a feathery brushstroke on the subject. To start with, however, I will say, that to the best of my knowledge, happiness is not something you can find, or gather, or achieve, at least not directly.

Happiness, I am sure, is the by-product of right behavior. Perhaps "calm" is a word that better describes what we are all really looking for, since in calm we will find happiness from time to time, whereas in agitation we never will. (Some of us find a kind of relief from our internal agitation by becoming involved in agitation in the outside world, but it's only a temporary distraction at best.)

I do believe that humans are designed to be happy as a general matter. I am coming to believe that, after biology is addressed (clinical depression, etc.), what usually gets in the way is the story/stories we tell ourselves and each other. If you listen, you'll hear a lot of people tell you, "Oh, I'm the kind of person who always…" or, "Oh, I'd never do such-and-such a thing…" These are the tools by which we keep ourselves on a self-perpetuating circle — what in fact is really meant by "karma".

If you spend, say, fifteen minutes a day just sitting and listening to your own mind chatter away, you'll probably start to notice some of these patterns in your own life. Try it for a week. Set a timer, and don't get up out of your chair unless one of the kids breaks an arm or some such. (BTW, you might not enjoy this at all at first, but hang in there. Must be present to win, you know.) As you become more familiar with the almost-automatic workings of your own head you might begin to detect the patterns that shut you down before you can enjoy what's going on.

I'm not one of those who say that everything is for the best. I am sure, however, that in any given situation, you have a range of options, and some of them are more conducive to calm than others.

No matter how bad the situation, it's always possible to worsen it, with a bit of effort. It's also possible to take the calmest approach, and I am sure that if you make that your effort, your plan of attack, you will find your life slowly becoming happier. Incidentally, you won't notice when you change over, but I do believe that one day you'll notice that you're happy enough.

I certainly hope so.[122]

*

Happy is a word with many definitions and connotations. It's also relative. In some ways, I'm *always* happy. In others, I'll *never* be happy.[123]

*

My goal is to become completely happy. I am progressing in this direction all the time, but every time a bad thing happens to me it leaves a wound, a wound that can only be submerged or expressed.

If it is *suppressed*, it affects my behavior always; if it is *expressed*, it is possible to get over it. If someone used to snarl at me, I would find myself snarling back until I could get off by myself and think, "Why did this person express anger toward me? Was *he* responsible for his feeling, or did *I* create the situation that made him express it? And if I met his anger with love instead of a snarl, wouldn't it make me feel better and happier instead of leaving me depressed and discouraged?"

More and more I try to meet anger with love. The world is love. Sooner or later everyone will love everyone else. That is the future. I think people are so hipped up on the point of view, us against them; it's all a hangover from the days of the left wing or fascism. It's not the way things are anymore; it's just us.[124]

*

OK, dear, let's go to work. Firstly, take on a different sort of writing task. Write down a history, year by year, of your life as you remember the most vivid moments. Write objectively. That is, describe what was said and done, not what you felt: no insults ("... and then that bastard said..." absolutely will not do.), no self-pity ("How could he treat me that way?" also will not do.). When you're done, then take some more paper and write down your conclusions about what each event meant. What I'm getting at here is to try to separate *what actually happened* from *what you understood it to mean.*

Remember for instance that it's not about being rejected, it's about your conclusions that you'd been rejected that matter. At this point in your life (now that you're in your 30's) it's okay to remember that the child you used to be *believed* that she had been rejected, but now what's important is not the rejection you feel happened TO you, but the rejectedness you carry withIN you.

(Meanwhile, as an aside, it's likely that the feelings of rejectedness you carry within might have set you up to be rejected in the more-or-less present as a result.) The more you see that it's your own belief that you are "rejectable" that informs your life, and the less you believe your troubles are a result of what happened to you as a child, the clearer your life will become and the more you will see things as they are, in and of themselves, and the less you will be controlled by your history. This, in turn, will go a long way toward generating a life that is calm and clear in the present.

Secondly, I recommend sitting in Zen meditation. The best book I know for that is *Zen Mind, Beginner's Mind,* by Shunryu Suzuki. It's all about watching your own mind rather than obeying it as though it were the infallible voice of the truth.[125]

*

I now realize that all men (and women) are born with the ability to be happy *naturally* — and that unhappy people are those who don't face reality and those who live a lie. I am not putting them down. Quite the contrary. I feel great tenderness and compassion for them and for all my fellow men and women. If each of us could pause for a moment or two several times during the day and just let everything "fall into place", we'd be much happier as individuals and as a nation.

That simple little practice — of *pausing, standing still and clearing the head of all foolish thoughts* — is as refreshing and invigorating as a good night of restful sleep. If you don't believe me, try it and you'll see.[126]

*

For me, [leaving The Monkees] never was a case of the bubble bursting. It was much more a case of leaving the bubble through the airlock as it slowly fizzled away. I only see this in retrospect. At the time, I wanted to get out because I wanted to be a Beatle-type musician. I wanted to lead my own band. I had no idea how difficult that was at the time. I just wanted to go off and do my own things. Now I wonder about my attitude then. I think it was probably a false attitude. On the other hand, if I'd been wiser, I might have left earlier. There's no telling. Like I say, I didn't have any sense of the bubble bursting. I just walked out of it. I mean, I had the bends for a while coming back into re-entry, but it wasn't like the bubble bursting in that I didn't have a sense that one moment everything was flying high and the next moment everything was miserable. Because I myself did not change my sense of contentment.

I found — and I have found consistently — that my sense of contentment has virtually nothing to do with my success. I was very content during certain periods with The Monkees. I was very happy at times, and I was miserable at times. I was happy afterwards sometimes, and I was miserable sometimes afterwards. And the history of my life has almost nothing to do — I'm talking about internal history, the history of my happiness — it has almost nothing to do with the history of my worldly success. So I didn't have any sense of the bubble bursting. It was just my life carrying on, step by step.[127]

*

I must say, with all due modesty and gratitude, that I am indeed happy. Usually, very much so. And even when I'm not really, really happy, I'm still aware that I'm a very lucky man and grateful for it.

I do believe, though, that happiness is not something you look for or try to have, but rather the result of doing your best to live right, which usually means being of service to others, and keeping to a high standard of behavior, to the best of your ability. AND, when you fall off the beam, make it right as best you can and get back on beam as soon as possible.[128]

Tork About How to do Life

There is always the miracle waiting around the corner. I can't guarantee that your dream situation is dialing your phone as you read this, but I know that some surprising things happen if one waits in faith, and, particularly, if one doesn't act out, running screaming from the house, for instance.

I wish I could be more concrete for you, but I have a lot of faith that things will work out for you.[129]

*

I have to say that the adjustments from one phase of my life and career to another have happened almost without my noticing it. I never made any preparations; I had no idea what I was getting myself into from one minute to the next, usually, so what could I do to prepare? I honestly don't believe anyone knows what's going to happen. How anybody prepares for the future (beyond a prudent financial plan) is beyond me. So, I guess my advice is, expect the unexpected, and roll with it to the best of your ability.[130]

*

The Sixties were a fabulous time for me, and I've had some ups and downs in my life, but mostly, the glamour and the glitz is gone, but the fabulousness of my life is still with me. I'm so glad to be where I am, and who I am, and in the state of health I am, and the age I am — all these things are still glorious.

It's really a function of being able to accept the health that I needed when I needed it, ultimately.[131]

*

I'd rather have nude swimming, it's much easier. There's a certain charge to bodies if they're covered up, and if you remove that, it takes a lot of that extra energy out of things.[132]

*

The most satisfaction in life everyday comes from being useful. I've been working really hard, gaining a lot of understanding, and when somebody else can use it, I'm a happy camper.[133]

*

Well, I am carrying around more [weight] than I want to, God knows, but I don't do too much about it. I have recently started to notice earlier and earlier and to be able to stop when I'd had enough to eat. I think the greatest mistake we can make in this arena is to eat because it's time, or because we're looking for something to do with our mouths and hands, or, particularly, when eating calms our jitters. I can't claim any kind of perfection in this area, but it does seem to be getting better, over the long run.

The only chocolate I eat is the dark stuff. That's supposed to contain anti-oxidants, and even to be good for your teeth. The same is NOT supposed to be true of milk chocolate, nor if you eat your dark chocolate while drinking milk. Milk seems to destroy the beneficial properties of the good stuff.

Mostly, though, I have to plead ignorance on this subject, because I come from a family that never had a great deal of trouble with weight. I mean, my mom put on a few pounds later in life, but it never seemed to make her uncomfortable, and my brothers and sister don't have a problem with weight, much, either. So I think it's just my jeans… No, no, I mean my genes.[134]

*

I'm not a rigid vegetarian. I eat much less meat than I used to because your nourishment must come from the sun and the ground, so we should go to the most direct source. When you eat a cow, you're eating the energy from the cow, not the grass, so eliminate the middle man.[135]

*

I went dead broke for a while. I still have my guitar. I sold my car, a 1967 MG, a couple of years ago. It was starting to rot away in storage.

Having had a solid taste of fame, I'm aware of the pitfalls of it. Being young enough to have assessed the experience and reevaluated my whole life on the basis of it, I've been able to see that what I once heard called "three hots and a cot" are my only requirements. Give me my meals, and a place to put my head at night, and I'm okay. That's all I really need, that and my community, my life with other people. To me isolation is the only sin. Human beings are not meant to live alone. And while I feel that I may have a fairly large place in the public life of the world today, it could be just a dream and a fantasy, and it certainly is not a fitting basis for my decisions. The basis for my decisions is to do what I have to do today, do what's put in front of me as well as I can, and to learn the lessons of the results.

What's happened to me in my life since then hasn't been so disastrous. I could have wished to have better financial resources at the present time, but so what? I've got my three hots and a cot and I have friends. I know I'm going to eat and I know I'm going to sleep and I know I'm going to have company. And I have a career, for Christ's sake. It's not tearing down the walls and breaking up the halls at the present moment, but I'm playing, I've got musicians – good guys, with lots of talent. I have no particular wants. I have odds and ends of desires running loose that may or may not ever be satisfied, but who cares? The really important stuff is right now, this very minute.[136]

*

The number of people who think they're self-made people, where did they get the energy to do it? Where did they get the tools to do it? Nothing comes from nothing. Maybe the Big Bang came from nothing, who knows, we have not got the information, but in earthly terms, in human terms, nothing comes from nothing.

There's a lovely lady, was my mum's best friend for years, is still happily living in La Jolla (CA), I went to visit her recently and she said, "You know, that way you are, that kind of funny, experimental, off-beat, you've been that way since, I knew you when you were two, you were like that."

And so, where does it come from? I can't say I *generated* that, I didn't *create* that, that's not *my* doing. And yet, whatever it was that came to the table through me — I'm the canal, so I get to watch it go on. And the same is true of everybody and everything.[137]

*

Well I think it's always two steps forward, three steps back in every endeavor. Maybe it's 99 steps forward, 98 steps back — I don't want to get too specific on the digits but there's always this back and forth, and back and forth, but I am hopeful that, in the long run, this is all going to settle down.

I believe that fundamentalist hate rhetoric and behaviors of all kinds are a direct outgrowth of that same fear. [If] I treat somebody nastily, they will treat somebody nastily in return — either in return, back to me, or in consequence to somebody else.

The number of people who are capable of saying, "Wait a minute, I don't have to do that," is very low. But it's *growing*. That number of people who say, "I get it. I get that what we're talking about is other people operating out of fear, I don't have to react fearfully."

That number of people is growing, we see that all over the place. The number of inspirational, spiritual publications, monthlies and books, is growing almost exponentially. Various other kinds of spiritual thought are becoming part of the everyday conversation.

If the New York Times says something about nirvana on its front page, then we've come a long way since what, the sixties or something like that — and I don't mean the group; I mean the religious concept. And I do believe that that is an expression of improvement, but fear raises its ugly head at every turn and it requires great patience and dedication to be able to...

I mean, I can't resist reacting fearfully a lot of the time at this point in my life. I'm getting better at it, like I said, it's a skill and I'm not terribly good at it yet, but I get the principles, which is a step up. Getting the principles is better than not having them.[138]

*

Never say never. Except sometimes. But only rarely say never, because if you never say never then you can't say never about never saying never, right?[139]

*

What challenges me the most? Right now it's actually the onslaught of the years. That is proving to be a big deal. As Bette Davis said, "Accruing the years is not for sissies." This one's a bear.[140]

*

It's OK [being 44]. Sure my knees aren't as wonderful as they used to be. But the other day I pounded down the pavement after a bus, and it felt like I was flying. Like I was eight.

Um. My back's going. My hair's falling out. I don't have any teeth left. My head fell off last night, which was kind of annoying. I left my spleen on a train last week. Basically, I'm falling to pieces but I feel simply wonderful.[141]

*

It's amazing how thrilling life has gotten now that I've learned how to live it. There are two kinds of pain — the pain from growing up and the pain from refusing to grow at all.[142]

*

I've noticed in my life that there are two kinds of pain in this life. One is the pain of growing up, and the other is the pain of refusing to grow up.

And the pain of growing up changes, and there's wonderful rewards attached to that — without drugs. And the pain of refusing to grow up is the same pain over and over and over again, and it never changes and there's no rewards.

But it seems easier to live without living, 'cos life is tough. It's a hassle to live. Life is a pain, sometimes, and [John] Lennon embraced the pain of his living. He struggled with issues like feminism, and struggled with his own sexism, and struggled with his own political understanding, and strove to learn his own humanity. And he worked like hell, he worked hard and he gave it all he had, and that's awful rare. So that's what made him special.

You know, when Elvis died, well, Elvis dies, you know, it's too bad, it's the death of a legend.

But when Lennon died, a warrior went down.[143]

*

The thing that is most important to me is that I haven't given up. I haven't quit. I haven't quit doing music, I haven't quit what we call the exploration of the mystery, I haven't quit trying to grow up, be as real as I can with my loved ones, I haven't quit. And I expect not to.[144]

Tork About Inspiring Stuff

No matter what kind of inspirational thing happens, somebody will latch on to one of the external details and call it that. It's called mistaking the finger for the moon. You point to the *moon* and somebody looks at the *finger*. It's inevitable.[145]

*

First of all, if you really love me, you'll do all your own thinking. You won't accept anyone else's belief as your own, or any of these images, unless you've thought it all out in your own mind. You won't believe anything you see or hear or read, whether it's about me or someone else, unless you've already got foundations for belief. And, if you ever read in some magazine, "Don't believe it unless you read it in such and such a magazine," *definitely* don't believe it! In other words, don't believe anything until you've been shown it to be absolutely true for yourself.[146]

*

Scary to cope, to have to deal, but sometimes it works out, gets real. Don't quit before the miracle.[147]

*

If you want to hear from someone who's older than you, you've come to the right place.

That "Don't quit before the miracle," which of course is not remotely original with me, is maybe one of the best general advises I have. (Can that be the plural of "advice"?) Another, which kind of is a bit more original with me, is, "Be a hero to yourself." By that I mean, regard your life's story in the same light as those tales of Greek and Roman heroes, who were born to kings and queens and found their lives dashed down to humble circumstances, and who redeemed their lives through heroic deeds (with a lot of help). Those heroic stories, it turns out, are everybody's stories, and it's deeply useful, I am convinced, to regard ourselves as that kind of hero.

Hang in there, and don't quit just before the miracle.

Heheheh.[148]

*

Sing out loud, mess up a bunch and laugh right out loud at yourself.

BTW, there will be no squashing sides of oneself on my watch, no suppressing the perfectionist. Rather celebrate another side of yourself, the lovable imperfect side, and let the perfectionist side be. That side has her virtues, too, and can be a good friend sometimes.

Keep rockin'.[149]

*

I regret to say that I can only claim the most modest of progress on the question [of procrastination] myself. It is, in fact, in some ways the greatest challenge in my life. What progress I've been able to make I owe to a self-acceptance I've been growing in. I am sure that the worse I treat myself the slower my growth is. I am, after all, a child of God (whatever that word may possibly mean to you), and I know that I was not assembled with insuperable evil built in. Therefore, I can deal with anything about my life I care to (certainly not everything; there's only so much time in one life, heheh).

As procrastination becomes a high priority problem, I deal with it as best I can, but I'm sure that my best chance of progress is accepting myself and trusting myself. This last one took a long time, even only to accept as a principle, never mind being consistent about practicing it.

Stick with yourself and stick with the winners. Your community will be your guide (if they're on your side, which you kind of have to check out), and with their help, you have all the tools you need to take care of — if not everything, then anything.[150]

*

It's not about "wrong". Your feelings are never wrong, let's start with that. Inappropriate maybe, damage causing maybe, but never wrong. Your feelings are what your feelings are, let's start with that.

You're all right, you're a human being, you're fine. Okay? Okay. That's a great starting point.

Now, the next question is: what's gonna lead you to a happier, better life? And I'll bet we got unanimity here. Stop a minute and think this through. See what's gonna happen if you let this go on.[151]

*

Most of us are defending some position. I am a good person, etc. Or, I am a terrible person, etc. These are positions that we defend. And those positions are like secondary shells that we lay outside ourselves — they aren't who we *are*. Every one of us is good and awful, has moments of behaving good and behaving badly. The real question is: who are we *underneath*? Stripping away those shells, seeing them for the illusions that they are, ultimately discovering who this one's self is underneath it all, is what this is really all about. In the bible it says: seek ye first the kingdom of heaven, and all will be added, [*But seek first the kingdom of God and his righteousness, and all these things will be added to you*. Matthew 6:33] and I think it's exactly the same thing to say: don't drink, make meetings, and your life will begin to come together.[152]

*

Believe in yourself at all times.

You won't believe in yourself at *all* times, but *pretend* you do.[153]

*

You never know where the help is going to come from, and there's always hope.[154]

*

It's impossible for any of us to *waste* time. We are where we are. If I sit rubbing my elbow, staring out into space, that's where I want to be, what I want to be doing. It's never a waste of time. Nothing is if you *want* to be doing it.[155]

*

Do not forget this moment… This is one absolutely perfect moment. And they happen too seldom in life. So, remember.[156]

Tork About Loneliness

I'm still coming to grips with the feeling that there is support for me in the outside world. I'm still relating on a day-by-day basis with my own loneliness and isolation. I've had some bleak moments, of course, and I'll continue to have them, but I trust that if I stay in contact with my source, that my bleakest moments will be a prelude and a vehicle to other times.[157]

*

Human beings are not built to do things alone. Alcohol feels great — for a little while. Fame feels great — for a little while. But in the long-term, going it alone doesn't work. I was baptized a socialist. My faith is in a community, and when you walk into a room full of rehabilitated people, it's like turning on a light switch. That's my faith.[158]

*

I'm not sure I'm very good with loneliness. I am finding that I am less and less lonely when I'm alone. This I must attribute to firmly taking myself in hand and, well, um, spreading the task around.

For one thing, I do divert a fair amount. I used to do it more than I do now (progress not perfection), but when I lived in LA, I'd pick a club at random some nights and go watch a band I'd never heard of. Or I'd take whatever paperback I was reading out to a coffee shop and sit for 90 minutes over a decaf Americano.

I spend a fair amount of time on the computer, reading news sites, emailing and doing some games and/or puzzles. (I do believe Sudoku improves my brain. I hope I'm not deluding myself.)

I call my friends on the phone and/or on instant messenger, complete with webcam now.

I also meditate, which greatly changes the dynamic of being alone. I don't sit in meditation as much as I believe to be good for me, but when I do, it becomes, like, my being alone is no longer a burden.

Finally, I remind myself that there are a lot of things I like to do that company feels like it interferes: working on my music on the computer, practicing guitar to a virtual rock rhythm section, reading, both time-passing and significant stuff.

And then, sometimes, no matter what, I'm lonely. Like I say, this is happening less and less over time. I have to attribute this, finally, to becoming more comfortable in my own skin. That in turn seems to come from being encouraged to do the right thing. My friends and support people are lining up more and more along the lines of, do respectable things, and you'll gain self-respect.

I wouldn't know of my own experience, but I hear that volunteering for church and community groups get you out of your isolation. If you try it and you like it, tell me, and maybe I'll try it, too.[159]

*

Pop entertainers in the '60s had no experience with fame. It takes a balanced personality, beyond that usually attracted to entertainment, to be able to handle it. I knew Jimi [Hendrix] and Janis [Joplin], and I know they both came to music out of loneliness. I once heard Jimi sing backstage, singing full out, like he never did onstage. When I told him it sounded great he gave me this embarrassed laugh, like a kid rejecting a compliment.[160]

*

I think that fame and celebrity is very much part of the process that is built into western society, as we understand it today, which separates people, one from another. I think that the basic thrust of society today is "individual distinctions among people", as opposed to the commonality, the community. And fame is one of the manifestations of it.

The famous and the rich are set apart as being different, something to strive for, something you have very little chance of achieving — something you have to pay a hell of a price to achieve. If you're willing to pay a hell of a price you can do it, but there's a hell of a price, and look how the mighty go down in flames.

And I think that we buy that. I think that Janis and Jimi and Jim Morrison bought it. Cass Elliot. Otis and the Big Bopper, Ritchie Valens, Buddy Holly, Rossington Collins, people who go down in flames. The price is too high.

I think this is a society of isolation and there is no school for fame.

If I had to take all of the *credit* and all of the *blame* for my own fame as an individual star — having made it on his own talent like Elvis — I think I would be dead today. I think that the difference between me, and that, is partly that I didn't care to partake on a personal level because as a musician I *resented* all the fame I was getting as an actor. I mean I had this barrier between me and my own fame. I wasn't taking all of it for real. And because I was in a group, sort of in a larger operation — and the group not only meant the other three guys, but also the producers, and the staff of the entire Monkees project, directors, writers, all of that, you know — so then I felt like I was a member of a team, and any success that was due me, was due to my coworkers in a much realer sense than maybe Elvis was allowed to feel. Nobody ever told Elvis, get yourself some "No" men. He never had anything but "Yes" men, apparently. So every single whim was supported and he had no feedback from the human community, from the plain working community, the common community, to tell him how badly he was veering off of the healthy and the whole and the complete and the real.

And I think the same thing is true of Janis, and Jimi, particularly because I knew those two and I saw some of what was going on with them. Jimi was an utter sweetheart on the surface when you get to meet him. He was kind and generous and open and attentive, and still there was something locked down deep inside. He never, ever displayed the passion of his music to me on a personal level, and still something was locked away. And Janis was struggling at both ends of it. She wanted to be part of everything, she wanted to be common blues woman, and she wanted to be separate and different and unique all at the same time.

Without people who understand, without people who have been through very much the same thing as one is going through, you don't have any sense of how you're going wrong. You have to steer by other people; that's all we have in life. And fame in general does not generate that. Fame generates the opposite. Fame generates isolation. Fame generates: you did it all right all by yourself, therefore your own instincts are going to be perfect right up until the end.

Janis. Jimi. Elvis. Show me different.

So that now, and I think that I have gotten involved with, and have help to create for myself, a community that is gonna keep me sane, so that if and when I strike to that same, anything remotely resembling that same level of fame, I'll have these private people that I can turn to, whose word I can trust, and I now know that it's better to hurt from having been wrong than to reject that hurt and die from the wrongness. Because I can hurt and I can survive it and I can go on to feel better from being right later on, from being correct in terms of the real humanity of things.

The question of why we shouldn't isolate, and why we're human, is the same kind of question as, why gravity? We're built that way, we're built as social animals.

This is my final discovery of the day. That we're built as social animals and not as individuals, the emphasis on individualism is really, terribly, terribly unhealthy, and it's responsible for, as far as I can see, that vast majority of present day discomfort, dismay and distress.[161]

Tork About Love

I'm a hand-holder. I'm not very big on expensive evenings in nightclubs, things like that. I'd much rather sit quietly with a girl, hold hands and talk. With five pairs of hands, I'd really have some business going! Now if I could only find enough girls who'd want to hold my hand…[162]

*

I think some girls are pretending to feel love for me which is really not love, even though they don't realize it. They direct their feelings and daydreams toward the image of me they see on the screen or in the magazines. Really, this is not love.

It's no good to just go about worshipping an image on the screen because, for one thing, that isn't really *me* they're loving because they don't really *know* me. They write words on paper saying, "Oh, I love Peter," but they don't love *Peter*.

The reason this just can't be real love is because if you're really in love, then it's all happening. You know it for sure because love is like a two-way thing all the time. Real love is totally returned. You can't really love somebody if they don't know you. This business of, "Oh, I'm in love with a boy who doesn't even notice I'm around and I love him so desperately that I dream about him at night." All you love is the image of somebody that you *want* to have, just to dream about him at night.

This can happen because girls may look around and not see what they want to see. They might see guys around who have something about them they don't like or who lack what they're looking for. Then they look at this picture of me, which has all the faults removed from it.

For instance, you'd never know if I had complexion trouble because it would all be under makeup. You'd never know if I were mean or angry unless you just happened to be in the way of one of my temper tantrums, which sometimes happens to fans. I sometimes lose my temper, like anyone, and if you happen to be in the way of it at the time, you might think, "Oh, what have I done?" You've done nothing. I was just being human.

Now, I don't think this loving of images is necessarily harmful, as long as those girls eventually find some other means of expression for their feelings. Nothing is harmful in itself, you know. Even smoking isn't desperately harmful if done with moderation. But you smoke a pack a day and you're almost sure to get cancer. So why do it at all? Why even bother to worship my image in the first place?[163]

*

Hysteria from the fans worries me. Even right here at this reception [in London] a girl just threw herself at me and said she loved me. My feeling is, if she really loves me, why doesn't she let me go when I ask her to?

Love should be a reciprocal thing, and a girl carried away by hysteria is not in love. Perhaps it is unrequited love, which is really just transferred emotions.

The thing that worries me most about fans is my lack of direct contact with them. The only contact I really have with them is through you, the press, and really that is not entirely satisfactory.

Occasionally we manage to get some letter reproduced in the fan club magazine, but that's as near as we get.[164]

*

It's important to remember, though, that love is mutually felt. There's no such thing as one person wanting another person more than that person wants him — that's an infatuation, or it might be called a hang-up. If I love a person and all that person does is keep turning her face away from me, again and again, all it proves is that I'm interested in having that person turn their face away from me. I'm interested in *not* getting what I want.

I believe that everybody always gets exactly what they want all of the time. That's why I believe that when somebody is constantly getting kicked in the face by someone they are supposed to be in love with, all it proves is that they're more interested in getting kicked in the face than in being in love. They're just hung-up.[165]

*

I used to live like Tarzan, swinging from vine to vine, but that's not the life of anything except "puer eternus" — the eternal child. That's not for me. I'm still very inclined to do very childish stuff. I fell, I got into this completely puppy love thing not too long ago. The woman was no good, but the puppy love was great![166]

*

I think I'm probably past the point in my life where finding the one and falling in love and agreeing to try to create something together is possible. On the other hand, it would certainly, you know, I would certainly love to have a companion that I thought knew me and understood me and with whom I could partner.[167]

*

Yes, I most certainly do [believe in love at first sight]! That does not mean that that's the only start to true love. In fact, it might not be the better way; it might deceive you into thinking that there is no more (or not much more) work to be done. I fell in love with one woman once the second I saw her. We had a lovely time together, but were obliged to part ways after some years. Then I met a woman whom I gradually — as opposed to suddenly — came to appreciate and love, and with whom I do believe (and hope) that I'm in my last relationship now.[168]

*

To Pam, my *sine qua non*.[169]

Tork About Michael Nesmith

Mike is the complete opposite to me except that we share the same religious beliefs — something I find very difficult to understand.[170]

*

I remember staying at Mike's house in Hollywood when we first started filming the series. It was the upper story of a two-story building on a little hillside. Mike's wife, Phyllis, was wonderful. Mike and I laughed a lot and played music together. I remember that time very fondly.[171]

*

Michael was very kind to me at the outset. He put me up through the entire shooting of the pilot. He and his wife had a wonderful little apartment just big enough for a guest on the day bed, which overlooked Hollywood.

Mike and I wrote a few things together. We were very comradely and very buddy buddy, and it was a wonderful time, with Mike's then wife Phyllis, and Christian, their little infant baby. The early days of the pilot shooting were just great by my lights and I had a wonderful time.[172]

*

I was playing banjo and he was playing guitar and a set of chord changes came out and it was a really rocking thing. So we wrote a banjo tune that we called the Monkee Breakdown. It's pretty good.[173]

*

I really get along with Mike best. He's married and enjoys his evenings at home with his family. My favorite date is to stop by his place, have some coffee, play cards, and listen to groovy music.[174]

*

Michael is really amazing. He really knows how to construct a joke. If the punch line isn't strong enough, he knows how to bring down the set-up so that it matches. The real key to humor is that the joke and the set-up match, and Michael knew how to master that.[175]

*

I have a great deal of respect for Mike as a musician and a songwriter. He's very good. He could make it on his own easily. Also he's one of the funniest people I've ever met.[176]

*

Well, I've never been really close with Michael for some reason. You know, I have a lot of respect for him and admiration. But somehow we've never integrated. We've never been warm with each other. We worked together and did pretty well at it really.[177]

*

Michael had his own way of controlling things. I don't think I can characterize it, he was just a manipulator and always ahead of the game and always knew how to push things around to make them happen. He pretty much kept himself in charge. I don't know *how* he did it exactly — If I knew how he did it, I would have done it myself, actually!

Michael, in my estimation, was never interested in the group being the musicians, except as a way-station to his own ideals, his own ambitions. He wanted to be in charge.[178]

*

Mike wants to be the boss. Basically Mike is, "My way, or the highway," and there's no room for discussion in his cosmos. And Mike basically didn't want to join the group. He wanted to be in charge.[179]

*

Having a voice in the recording process was for me to say, "I belong to this." For Michael, it was about power. Michael came from an extremely poor situation. He told us that his mother would boil up a batch of Liquid Paper on the stove and he would go to Dallas and sell it, and they would eat that night on what he made that day. So it was pretty close. And so for Michael, it was about making sure everything was under control.[180]

*

There were times when we just couldn't tolerate each other.[181]

*

He behaved imperiously a lot. I thought, I think. I don't know what it was. Mike was kind of, I think, acerbic, like acidic. He had this kind of lemony bitter… I want to say acidic, it sort of is like that, it's a texture. He gave off this vibration of being sour and he was abusive. He would never like anything that he hadn't brought up.

One day Micky and I were playing guitar, and I hit on this rhythm on the guitar that sounded real good to me and Micky. And we said, "Mike, listen to this."

And he said, "Uhh…"

And I think, again, that it was important to him that the attitude that he conveyed, it was more important to him to convey that attitude than whatever the real one was. I don't believe that it was necessarily a real attitude, or rather that it wasn't necessarily his taste. If he'd come across it in the first place he might have thought it was wonderful. That the circumstances of its being presented to him, ie., by somebody else, supposedly a peer, made it totally unacceptable to him.

It was almost nothing. He couldn't have said, "Hey, that's nice." He had to say, "Uhh, it's ok."[182]

*

I didn't have the fight with Mike. Boy, I don't know what I would have done, cause I think he was pretty strong... We were shooting a Western sequence, can't remember which one, we were supposed to come out of a hotel backwards, guns blazing, and we had 45's and they had blanks in them. Blanks shoot these wads of paper, and they sting. If they hit you, they hurt like hell, you're supposed to take great care not to shoot *at* anybody, cause you can hit them and sting them, and if it hits them in the eye or in the ear, it can do them some damage.

And after the scene, Mike came raging at me, saying that I'd shot him with the blanks. And this is toward the end of a long day, and it was unbelievable, it was infuriating, and I was in tears about it. And I wouldn't go back to shooting. I wasn't going to resume shooting until... it was either him or me, we just weren't gonna be on the set together, just wasn't gonna resume any more shooting.

And Michael finally came back and got me and said, "This is silly, you don't have to feel..." He didn't say he was *sorry*, he just said, "Look, don't feel bad for feeling bad."

So I went back to shooting. But I resented him, boy, for a long time.

We didn't punch each other out. [Did I feel like it?] Yup. Yeah, he made it sound as though he was gonna duke it out with me. And I can't get into a fight if I know a fight's coming, for some reason. The only reason I got in it with Davy is because it happened before I knew it, and then I was angry. But with Mike, he said, "All right, now I'm gonna punch you out because of what you did," and I couldn't take that, that just breaks me up, I have no idea what's going on.

[I got to beat up everybody except Mike.] Isn't that wrong? He was the one I should have beaten up![183]

*

He never apologized. Michael never apologized. About anything. At any time. Under any circumstance. As far as I know. Whatsoever. I mean, I don't know about his marriages, but …[184]

*

One of the producers asked me if I would stay if he fired Mike Nesmith.

I told him, "No."[185]

*

He's always been the question mark. Mike has, and had, other ambitions. He's giving what he's got to this. He's here and he's committed, and you can see it. He's not holding anything back on this tour, nor the last one. He has other things he wants to do. But he's not going, "I can't stand this; I've got other things to do." Michael isn't doing that. The result is I sense a lot of commitment from him on this. We're getting along brilliantly.[186]

*

Mike and I have been back and forth with the emails […] I bore him no ill-will. I have a lot of respect and admiration and some affection for Mike. And I'm glad to be back in touch with him.[187]

*

Michael is deserving of an enormous amount of respect, as far as I'm concerned; he's a man of extraordinary accomplishment.[188]

Tork About Micky Dolenz

When I first met Micky I thought he was nowhere. I thought he was right out of Reader's Digest. He seemed to be everything I stood against: second-hand humor, second-hand situations, everything. I thought, well, they hired him because they needed someone with professional experience. Period.

You see, when Micky was in Circus Boy he didn't have anyone at all around that was his age. His whole life was spent in pleasing adults — it was the heaviest experience of his life. So that affected him a lot.

Then I got to know him and he grew and evolved and got bigger and bigger and bigger. He just didn't stop growing and now I think he's a full-fledged genius. He's really one of the brilliant people of our time.[189]

*

Micky had no real sense of humor when we first got together. He developed it. All of his jokes came from The Readers Digest. I don't normally read The Reader's Digest — I normally read things in their entirety, complete with their complexity — but it just so happened that that was the magazine in my piano teacher's waiting room. So I knew all his jokes. Suddenly he turned around and decided he knew how to be funny, and he's now one of the funnier men around.[190]

*

Micky was the lynch pin of The Monkees. As a visual comedic group, it was Micky who could go nuts, and who could trip out and deliver the lines. He was a genius when he was in his element.[191]

*

Micky has a practical side that he tries to hide behind his jokes and imitations, but it's there nevertheless. I'm not practical at all, so I admire this in him. He's got his business affairs in order at all times and knows just what happens to all his money and things. I never do. I can't keep track of how much money I have with me at a given time.[192]

*

I used to say things like, "Micky, don't you know that that's not right? It has to be this way." And he'd tell me, "No, man, that doesn't matter." Well, after a while I discovered that he had been *right!* Whatever it was, he had been right and I'd been wrong. That's the sort of thing that really got me thinking. His attitude would have seemed to be so wrong to me, yet I'd find out that it was so right. I'd get overwrought over nothing.

Then there would be something that I wouldn't think was worth much and he'd be fascinated. I'd tell him, "What's the matter with you? Man, you're hung up on the wrong kind of thing." And he'd tell me, "No, man, this is where it's at." Well, *again* he'd turn out to be right.[193]

*

We were all exhausted in Chicago. We should have been resting between shots, with 30 cities in 40 days, and syncing, we had to shoot some sequences in between times. It was awful, really grueling. And tempers were really tight. We didn't want to be making those damn shots on the road in between concerts, when we should have been able to relax and go someplace. Mick was sitting at the drums and we were syncing a number, I don't remember what number it was, but it was one of those numbers with the colors fanning out behind us and in front of us with that backdrop.

We did a bunch of tunes against that backdrop, and we were in a break in the shooting. Micky was sitting behind his drums, fuming. He was really ready to just blow his cork someplace and somewhere. And I had a flashcube, and I tossed it ever-so-gently in the air — and I knew he was really in a mood to explode — and it hit him on the shoulder. And he looked at me, and he glared, completely out of control and threw his drumstick at me with all his might.

I knew he was gonna do that, too, and I ducked. He missed me. And then we were in the clinch, and along came Rafelson.

And Rafelson said, "Boys, Boys! God's sake, boys, boys!" And we stopped. Right then and there, we didn't fight anymore. We just came out of it, and we pretended like we'd been pretending, just to put Rafelson on.

He said, "Oh, God! You guys scared me so bad!"[194]

*

Micky is too wild for me. Sometimes we go bowling or surfing together. But Micky likes to make a lot of noise, and that always attracts people and autograph hounds. It embarrasses me.[195]

*

We never hung out together. We often visited each other in the early days, you know, invited each other to our parties, and I went over to Micky's all the time. We talked a lot about helicopters and atomic energy and the Heisenberg Principle, and he had a great little recording studio and we actually wound up making a record in his recording studio, a splendid little record I think.[196]

*

God, I remember when Micky showed me ["Randy Scouse Git"] – I was so excited. (He) played me the verse, and he played me the chorus, and he said, "And then at the end we do them both at the same time!"

Wow, that was a brilliant piece of music. I've always thought that Micky was far more creative than he ever gave himself credit. I always thought that song was proof of it.[197]

*

Micky's major character flaw in my book is that he is afraid to revisit where he has done well. He wrote "Randy Scouse Git" and he never again went into heavy psychedelia. He was willing to take the beginner's luck that came to him. He's a brilliant guy, and he's willing to let his brain loose and flash out and act in unknown territory. But once he's done something good, he knows that his next three, five, eight efforts won't be as good because they won't have that newcomer's charge. So if he never goes near them again, he avoids the disappointment of not being able to do as well again, or at least for a little while, and then accumulate the skills it takes to do better, and then go ahead and be brilliant beyond that. If Micky were willing to do that, I think he would be one of the world class artists of the day.[198]

*

You know he was really out there, Dolenz. One of my great regrets is that he wasn't able to credit himself for his own creativity. That to me is one of the great tragedies of the history of The Monkees. Maybe the single greatest tragedy, aesthetically anyway.[199]

*

It's been a lot of fun tramping the boards with Micky. We laugh every night, out loud suddenly, spontaneous laughter at what's going on with each other. One night we were doing "Stepping Stone" and I was doing the deep crouch with the tongue flashing in and out, and Micky's looking at me going, "Oh, gross!" And we laughed like crazy. And the next night, Micky was doing it, and I tapped him on the shoulder and I wiggled my finger at him, as if, you know, *Don't do that*, and he looked a little abashed, and we laughed like hell. We never know which one of us is going to take which end of which joke, if not something new, so it's a lot of fun, every night is a new adventure.[200]

*

Micky… I enjoy hugely. We have some very good times together. We laugh a lot. We pay attention to what each other is doing on stage and so there's communication there. Micky's always been a lot of fun.[201]

*

Micky's very easy to hang with. We get into flights of political discussions and we talk about subatomic physics, to the extent that either of us know anything about it. He's great to talk to. I have a lot of fun with him and always have.[202]

*

I'm just delighted to be onstage with [Micky and his always great voice]. You know, that my fortunes are such that I'm allowed onstage with that is a true blessing in my world.[203]

*

He's so f-ing funny I can't believe it sometimes.[204]

Tork About Money

If money is a concern, well, then, money's a concern. There's nothing wrong with striking out for serious independence if there is a concern about being left without resources. I hope, however, that that concern is not the overriding be-all and end-all of your considerations.

Money is, of course, critical to civil well-being in this life, but beyond a certain point, more does not improve the quality of life… much. If there seems to be a useful, satisfying career open to you, then follow it unless you're deeply concerned that you won't be independent there, in which case maybe the next more lucrative career path is better for you.[205]

*

Course now there isn't a terrible money problem. Some folks think I must be throwing money around. Not true, really! And anyway there's a lot to be said for being poor. I don't mean poor like you don't get enough to eat. But for a musician, for a singer, there's a lot in *having* to work for your bread and butter, it keeps you on your toes. You learn by experience and you get deeper experience if you are dependent on your work enabling you to keep from starvation. That's why those early days in Greenwich Village were so important to me. That's why, I guess, I still go back there whenever I can.[206]

*

The thing I miss most about the times before I was a Monkee is poverty. Money has both advantages and disadvantages, and the main disadvantages is that it ties you down.[207]

*

The weight and speed and the gush of attention is inhuman. It is beyond the capacity of anybody to absorb. It's one thing for a banker to work his way up to the point where he's making hundreds of thousands of dollars a year. It's another thing to make a million-five in two years after having lived on fifty dollars a week.[208]

*

I gave a lot of my money away when I was younger – just left it in bowls around the house and people would help themselves to handfuls of it. I wasn't thinking too clearly at the time and it might have been my low self-esteem, thinking that I didn't deserve to keep the money, but it wasn't really that bright, was it? I mean, there's nothing wrong with giving money away to people, but give it where you can do some good.[209]

*

I think I was a sort of Gatsby. I was isolated and did not have a continuing sense of community. I'd have a moment of friendship here or there, a moment of sharing, but I didn't believe that was the main body of my life. I didn't know who my friends were, and anytime somebody asked me for a favor I wrote them off as a hang-around. And I wasn't able to ask people for favors, because I was supposed to have all that it took to keep myself together, because I had the money. At the same time, by giving the money away, I thought I was returning something to the community. I didn't see myself as apologizing, which is how I see myself now. But I had all this money, and I tried to make amends to the world by throwing it at people. And, essentially, what that did was to isolate me all the more.[210]

*

The big bosses just put The Monkees' name on a lot of our recordings and then showered us with praise when they became a hit. I was called into a mass interview to become a Monkee and was told to cut out any bad habits — like smoking grass. When I wanted to publicly protest America's involvement in Vietnam I was told to keep quiet. Two of the guys who controlled us were Bob Rafelson and Bert Schneider, who have become big-time movie people now. I don't blame any of them. It's the system. They wanted us to get their fortunes. And I enjoyed the ride. I got to see the world and meet my own idols. But everything is so fast. I got ripped off all the time. We had limos and thousands of fans and teen magazine interviews. But they were all bullshit — they never printed anything but crap. I even got ripped off when I went to buy a house. When the real estate people see a teen idol coming, they know it's easy money. They jack up the prices. You don't know anything, so you're exploited. The whole entertainment business is about fraud. I found that even my idols, like Jimi Hendrix and Janis Joplin, had to play the merchandising game. They had to become products to make the mark.[211]

*

I either didn't notice, I didn't care, or I didn't permit it. It was that easy, generally. I only know in retrospect how badly I was ripped off. Largely financially. I let it happen to myself. You know what they say about a fool and his money.[212]

*

I think I was imbued with the notion, as my money ran out, that my fate was not in my own hands. I didn't have the sense that I had to hold on to it because nobody was going to save it for me.[213]

*

David [Crosby] let me have his — well, not his apartment — he had a house, and David let me stay there for most of a year. It was sort of by way of interest on the loan [of $25,000] I gave him to buy his boat, and I stayed there with my then girlfriend, and our daughter was born in that house.[214]

*

A lot of conjectures were realized, not exactly dreams. What was realized: I actually made and spent real money. Now that's a realization, you know? All that money as a realization, that's really something.

It was very interesting, I'd heard all the stories, flash in the pan successes who make a lot of money and then go down the tubes. I said, "This isn't going to happen to me. No, not me."

But as a matter of a fact, I did not learn how to save my money, and I didn't know how to spend it either — if I'd known how to spend it, at least I'd have had some more tangible result. The results I did have are almost entirely intangible, that is to say, there's a lot of people walking around who spent some very, very stoned times that they otherwise would not have spent. Although some of these people, I think, were professional finders of money. And suckers-up of other people's well-being.

Basically, the truth is, I had no serious, competent, concerned, involved, professional money help. I did have some management, but it either was not involved with me personally, or did not stand to gain by my financial success. In other words, the management of The Monkees operation, the less money I made, the more they made, so our financial interests were divergent. Every penny they paid me came out of their pocket, right? The people who had financial interest, whose financial interest paralleled mine — my money managers — did not have any understanding of my professional situation. They were a good and competent crew, and I don't have too much to say against them apart from they did not know how to cope with the flash-in-the-pan type of success. They were accustomed to dealing with people who made their money long and slow and hard over the long haul.

I had some great fun. I did make some awful lot of records on my own account, which I never would have had the chance to do. They just said, "Go ahead in the studio!"

I didn't even know I was paying for it at the time! Afterwards I found out.[215]

*

One thing is clear: there is a much higher joy in service than there is in acquisition of wealth. (Remember that it isn't money that's the root of all evil, it's the *love* of money.)[216]

*

It was actually a relief when it all faded. It meant you could actually count on your friends again; you knew the people who came around were people you could count on. I don't think human animals should go through that shock. It took me 12 years to recover from it. Of course, it was some fun — it wasn't all bad. When the cameras are rolling, you do your best with all your heart and it could be a lot of fun.[217]

*

There's a lot of things involved with money and recognition, and the price was much higher than I expected. There's an isolating pressure that goes along with success. I couldn't handle it.[218]

*

I did make a pretty fair amount of money with The Monkees. Not much by today's standards, but a pretty fair amount. But I let it all go because I didn't understand value then. I didn't understand value in myself. What I've learned since then is you can't handle money well if you don't have an appropriate sense of self-value.[219]

*

I don't need money. Money doesn't mean anything to me. If you can't be happy poor, you can't be happy rich.[220]

Tork About The Monkees

I think people who preferred Peter Tork to the others were people who did not know if they belonged in life or not. The other three as characters were so self-assured, you believed that they didn't have a problem. If you saw yourself as having a problem with life, you probably went for the Peter Tork character. Offbeat. Not quite mainstream. Somehow not quite in tune.[221]

*

So I was walking down the street, I think I was on the lower east side, and between steps, I was informed, I was struck, I was suddenly under orders, there was no doubt about it, I didn't hear anybody say anything in English — or any other language for that matter, not that I understand any others — it was not in *words* but the content was, I experienced it as undeniable, irrefutable and true, and it was: "Get out of town. You have to leave town. You have to leave New York."

And I said, "Okay. I'll settle my affairs and as soon as I find a place to stay, and a ride, I'll go to either Los Angeles or San Francisco, whichever comes up first."

A girl from a visit I made to Washington DC called and said, "Hi, I'm in Long Beach, right in Los Angeles county, I just came out here, you can stay here if you want."

Then I walked into a bar and couple of people I knew said, "We're driving out to Los Angeles, you want to come?"

You know, I'm not prepared to figure out what it was, it could have just been some gut feeling out of the blue, it might have been angels, it might have been the voice of Jehovah himself of maybe the Buddha… I don't know, but I'm just telling you what I experienced.

So I got in the car and off we drove and I landed in Southern California in the middle of '65.[222]

*

Then Steve [Stills] called me on the telephone, "Peter, I just met a guy who is producing a TV show based on *A Hard Days Night*. You should go try out."

"Yeah, yeah. What about you?"

"Well, they liked me well enough, but they thought my hair and teeth would not photograph well, would not be telegenic, and did I know anyone who *looks* like me with *one-tenth* my talent… and I thought of *you*, Peter."

He's so jealous, he had to settle for CSNY, he's never forgiven me.[223]

*

There were a number of events leading up to it that lead me to think that there was a certain kind of ordained quality to it all. I'm not a mystic, by any chance, but I've seen a lot of connections occur that standard, conventional, Western logic isn't large enough to take in. And I believe that this was pretty much set up somehow. It's almost as if I had no choice. Things sort of occurred. For instance, Stephen Stills called me and said, "Go try out." And I said, "Yeah, yeah, yeah," and hung up and left and didn't think about it.

Well, he called *again*. Nobody's ever called me with a suggestion like that *twice*. Not before, not since.[224]

*

I think I saw that Monkee walk in a Cary Grant and Murna Loy movie once.[225]

*

I did as well as I knew how and have nothing to be ashamed of. The most significant thing about The Monkees as a pop phenomenon is that we were the only TV show about young adults that did not feature a wiser, older person. We were out to throw off the shackles of an outmoded authoritarianism that was full of lies — and still is.

Our music may not have been daring, but the TV show was and deserves at least a footnote in history on that account.[226]

*

When The Monkees first aired, it was the first time on network television (in the days when there were only three networks) that a group of young adults was presented as being in charge of their own lives, without a "wiser" senior adult figure directing or advising them. I've spoken of this before. In the wartime tumult of the 60's political and social change it was clear to many of us young adults that a great many figures in authority were not a reliable source of information or direction. Every Monday night, viewers tuned in to watch "four crazy boys" muddle through on their own and come out all right by the end of the half hour. The show was both a benign break from the carnage on the world stage and a reflection of a shift (introduced with the Beatles' *Hard Day's Night*) that we, as a generation, were called to account for our own truths, our own lives, our own destinies.[227]

*

As the years have rolled by, I've come to appreciate [my past] I think fairly. It wasn't the Beatles, but there was a very important aspect to the whole time in the movement, and The Monkees TV show brought it through television and to those who otherwise might not have heard it. And it was this, it was a time that might have been thought of as anarchic but the reason for that was that there was no authority worth paying attention to. Johnson and Nixon were the Presidents and they were bogus. They were absolutely without moral authority, and we were thrown on our own. The characters on that situation comedy were without authority, without adult figure. We did it ourselves because we *had* to, you couldn't count on Johnson and Nixon. Echoes of the present age.[228]

*

My personal belief is that Bob [Rafelson] is an evil-minded man. He likes to bring people down. Bob was often unsupportive as a human being and distinctly negative — and I was on the short end of that.

There's one example [in the film, *Head*] — where Ray Nitschke, the football player, keeps hitting me. He was a Hall of Famer for the Green Bay Packers. He's doing his best to hit me but not to give it all he's got because if he does, I'm a squashed bug. So this guy's one of the toughest men in football, he's coming at me and I'm scared [but] figure it's good to be scared because that's what an actor should do.

But Bob goes: "Ha, ha! Look at Peter! He's scared! Ha, ha!"

I was just about ready to kick him in the balls. It was like, *For fuck's sake, Rafelson! You're making fun of me 'cos I'm scared? How do you think that's going to affect the quality of your movie, pal?* I was so angry!

That's the style in which he damaged what could have been a fulfilling quality experience.[229]

*

When I recorded "Can You Dig It," the guitar solo originally ran about three or four minutes all by itself. We cut that back to a minute and a half. Bob Rafelson took a pair of scissors and snipped off the end of it. He didn't ask me to shorten it, which I would have been glad to do. He just chopped it off. Son of a bitch! I have a lot of gripes about that, but that's neither here nor there.[230]

*

I must say the one I was most impressed to be playing with was Lon Chaney, Jr. He had the most impressive credentials, as far as I was concerned, particularly when you include his heritage; his father, Lon Chaney, Sr., was the great Man of a Thousand Faces. We don't see his work too often anymore, since he worked in the silent era, but he was one of the greats of all time. Jr., in addition to the glory of having been on a Monkees episode, was the great star of *Of Mice and Men*.

You mentioned Reginald Gardiner, whom I cast in the episode I directed, "Monkees Mind Their Manor." He, of course, was a delight to work with. We mustn't forget Ann Marie, who worked with us twice! There were more, too, than I can safely name who became bigger stars after they played on The Monkees. But the guy who was the favorite on the set has to have been Stan Freberg. He was as wild on the set as he was on screen. I grew up practically venerating Stan Freberg as the master satirist. He did about five satires on the old Dragnet radio show alone! Some of his riffs became bywords on the set after he left, particularly a quick, dry "Don't do that!" at odd moments, which cracked us up.[231]

*

The producers would make cuts so that the show flowed to their liking, and we were sometimes a minute short, so we started doing impromptu bits, which evolved into us scheduling time for segments with people we knew and respected. I had hoped to bring Janis Joplin on, but it never worked out.[232]

*

Well, it's fascinating to find out that there are kids today who are fans of The Monkees and of mine. And of course, you ask me what I think of [the fans]? I'm not going to tell you they suck.

The songs have lasted for the same reason that we love music from earlier decades and even centuries; the good stuff is recognizable forever. I am totally psyched to have been a part of making that fabulous song book, certainly one of the top ten songbooks of the pop and rock era.[233]

*

I'd taken music theory, I knew how to write a counterpoint. I wrote a counterpoint.

"Oh, that's very nice, Peter... *this* is the record. This is the record. We're adding the lead vocal now and then it will be done."

They take an idealistic hippie out of the Village and put him in the middle of the hard, crass, cold world of commercial record making and something's gotta give. And something certainly *did* give. It was murder, I don't how I stood up to it. As a matter of fact, I didn't. I really think that I had a pretty serious collapse finally from the whole thing.

Right then and there I developed what you might call a small resentment, and I started to go a little crazy. And I think I made my views known.[234]

*

It was Michael who destroyed it for us. We were irritated — Michael and I particularly — about the way the records were being made because we weren't included, we weren't in the loop.

Now I look back on it and I see that it was absolutely necessary — if I'm going to make a TV show about a bunch of rock and rollers and I'm taking four unknowns off the street, I'm not trusting them to make records! Who knows what disasters can occur. I'm going to get the pros. And that's what they did, they got the pros in there. Or the prozac! So they made the records without us.

And being kids at the time, I didn't get it. And Michael, being the kind of person who wants to be in charge of all things at all times, (Davy and Micky thought it was okay because that's the way actors did records) so Michael and I were upset about that. And Michael spilled the beans. He said, "Call us fake because, by God, we are!"

And like sharks to blood, the press went right to it and that was the end for us.[235]

The reason I went along with it is because I never took any initiative of anything on my own account. I basically did whatever, wherever I was pointed.

Stephen [Stills] said, "Go try out," I tried out. They said, "Come here, do this," I did that. "Sign here," I signed there.

And really, I'm only recently now getting to the point in my life where I'm beginning to say, "Let me figure this out. What is it that I really want? What steps do I have to take?" And even then I have to recognize that I have no control over events, all I can do is say, "This is the kind of thing that I'd like, and this is the kind of thing I have to do to make my chances better." And then I do that, and then I have to just let the results be whatever they are. As a matter of fact in some ways that was one of the problems when I broke up with The Monkees; I left because I couldn't get those guys to get back into the studio to do the same kind of thing that we'd done on our third album. Which was Micky on drums, Michael on guitar, me on piano, our producer on bass, Davy Jones playing rhythm sections and then hiring an occasional string player, something like that.

Micky said, "You can't go back." I think he thought he was Thomas Wolfe. And Davy said, "I don't want to be banging a tambourine day in and day out, you guys. It takes you 54 takes to get your parts down, I've got my part down first take." He's banging a tambourine! So we went into a mixed mode, but I wanted to be a real live group, I had this Pinocchio-Gepetto complex. And when they wouldn't go for it, it burned me out, and there I was being burnt out because things wouldn't happen my way, and it was a case of his majesty the baby trying to have his own way. If I'd had the good sense God gave me I might have noticed that I *was* having my own personal way — in the sense that what I wanted for myself was what was happening: I could be in the studio playing bass or guitar or piano on every single cut The Monkees did from then on if I wanted to. But that wasn't enough for me.

I thought it was more honest, I thought it was a bigger deal, I wanted a real live group, I thought this was the way things were done, and I was the victim of the same illusion that other people were criticizing us for shattering in their lives. In other words: "You don't do this all by yourselves, you're not an organic group, and how could you, and you've broken my heart." As if we'd broken their hearts, as if it wasn't the shattering of false illusions — if you hang on to false illusions, of course your heart is going to get broken.

And when [Mike and Micky and Davy's] reasons changed, and their behavior changed, and my plan didn't change, I went after them screaming to try to mend my shattered illusions. What a jerk!236

*

Davy's arm got tired. He got sick of banging the tambourine all day long. And Micky lost faith in himself. He never did believe he was a decent drummer, so he didn't want to do it anymore. Mike wanted to produce his own records. He wanted to have total control. I was the only one who believed in the group per se, and so there I was all by myself, wanting a group, with nobody to be a group with.237

*

Micky did a great job [drumming] on *Headquarters*. [But] he wasn't going to do it again, and there was nothing you could do [to change his mind]. We had to go back in the studio. He said, "Peter, you can't go back."

Eddie Hoh did the drumming [on *Pisces, Aquarius, Capricorn & Jones Ltd.* – save for "Cuddly Toy"]. Chip [Douglas] got him 'cause he could read [music]. The result is that you get directed stuff, there's no group interaction, which is why I wanted the group to be on the album in the first place. You listen to Beatle albums and one of the things that makes them great is that they have found ways to use who they have to get what they want without asking anyone to do what they couldn't do. That's what makes group music happen. That's all I ever hoped for, and I had it for like a minute on *Headquarters*.[238]

*

I had my conditions. I didn't submerge myself in The Monkees as they stood. I wanted to submerge myself in The Monkees as I'd hoped they'd be. The reason I became disenchanted and left is because we did do what I'd hoped we'd do, which was make an album together (*Headquarters*), and there was no follow-up album.

I thought we were capable of being a hit musical group as well as a TV show cast, and I had hopes of our doing that. But in fact, the personnel weren't right, because none of the other three wanted that; only me. That left me out in the cold.[239]

*

The best *natural* musician in the bunch was Davy. He never hit a bad note. My pitch is not as certain, Micky's isn't as secure. Mike's is, but he doesn't have the emotional range Davy had. Davy could sing Broadway, ballads and rock. He could do anything. What I am, among these guys, is the best trained, the only one who could read and write music. Michael wrote the horn and cello part to "Shades of Gray." He wrote it in his head, he sang it to me, and I notated it, and I notated it for the French horn. I'm the only one of the four of us who was in possession of that body of information. I took piano for six years and French horn for a couple, plus music theory in college.

And Micky is one of the better pop singers of all time. Not too long ago, I told him, "You must be one of the top twenty pop singers of all time." He said, "Twenty?" I said, "OK, fifteen." He said, "Fifteen?" I said, "OK, ten, but that's my best offer."

And Mike Nesmith is extraordinarily rigorous in pitch and time. And he's got imagination, and he's a very hard worker. I'm not. The only thing I have going for me is that I'm trained.[240]

*

There's some frustration there [that the other three guys sang most of the songs], but in retrospect, I can see I wasn't the guy for most of those things. I did do the one song, "Your Auntie Grizelda," during the first two albums. On the second album, I had a few lines here and there, and I shared a lead vocal with Micky on "Words." I think there's a song or two I might've done as well or better than the other guys because of the dramatic meaning of the song. There's a song on *Headquarters* called "Early Morning Blues and Greens." I look back and I think, I should've fought to do that song. It has me written all over it, and I should've been the guy who sang it.[241]

*

I'm getting better at it these days — but in those days I was almost entirely unable to fight for what I saw as quality. If I didn't get somebody fighting on my behalf then it just didn't come to pass. And none of the other guys was much interested in supporting my sense of quality, they had their own agendas and each one of them… I mean, not that I was left out in this regard, no one of us really supported any of the others, except that I like to think that I tried to support Micky in a way which, for some reason, he never did pick up on. I mean, I think that Micky has a certain kind of genius that he was never able to acknowledge in himself. But be any of that as it may, I just basically think that I wasn't feeling a part of it anymore already by that point, I'd already felt like I was odd man out, and of course I quit almost immediately thereafter. In fact, I think it's *The Birds, The Bees & The Monkees* that has some tunes that were recorded after I quit.242

*

Part of me was in the middle of The Monkee thing, and part of me was outside it, isolated from it. The Monkees' records were for teenyboppers and the instrumentations were deliberately non-threatening. Everybody said The Monkees were a plastic pop group, I guess because we became known through television. But nobody said anything about the creation that was the Mary Tyler Moore or I Love Lucy shows. No TV shows were judged by that standard.243

*

How did my family relate to the fact that I was a Monkee? I don't know too much, they didn't talk much about it. You know, when I got the gig they were congratulatory, but the kids used to come and rip up pieces of their lawn and things like that. They had to un-list their phone number because they were getting harassing phone calls for years on end, but I don't think they related at all, generally speaking. My brothers and sister related much more seriously, particularly later.

One brother of mine said to me, "You know you're part of Americana now."

And I guess, yeah, I guess that's true enough.244

*

My brother looks at me in wonder. He says, "You know, it really is amazing that The Monkees became a part of America, ingrained, part of the fibre."

It's strange to be part of that, to look back on that whole time, and see myself as having partaken of that, you know?

Half of me goes, "Do I deserve it?"

And the other half of me says, "Shut up! Don't ask! Deserve, shmerve!"[245]

*

It is mind-boggling. I'm all agog. I didn't think I was going to live to be 50, much less celebrate the 50th anniversary of some fly-by-night explosive but temporary pop phenomenon — which is what everyone figured we were going to be. I mean people from other TV shows get to go to those autograph shows and I see them all the time. But they are not performing any more. They don't draw crowds like we do. It is actually stunning.[246]

*

We were getting along pretty well until I had a meltdown. I ticked the other guys off good and proper and it was a serious mistake on my part. I was not in charge of myself to the best of my ability — the way I hope I have become since. I really just behaved inappropriately, honestly. I apologized to them.

I'm sure [alcohol] played a part, but I cannot honestly say it was anything more than a very slight part. It could have been very, very minor. But the main thing was that I had a meltdown and I messed up.[247]

*

Infighting?
Oh no, we always fought right out loud!²⁴⁸

*

For all of the potential shortcomings that have spun us apart, I have to pay tribute to each of them, separately and together, for just being magnificent talents. I only wish that we could have explored the talent we had better and longer and more efficiently.²⁴⁹

*

Now it's fun and good times and good show business. Our personalities have changed a lot. Micky and Davy have mellowed enormously. We're much more comfortable together. Actually they're very talented guys. And they're crafty show biz people. I'd be happy if I could live my life doing Monkees' shows three or four months a year, my own stuff for several months, and then writing and relaxing the other months.²⁵⁰

*

Micky and Mike and I have a very cordial relationship and share a lot of common topics. We go to lunch together when we're all in town and have a good time. I love and respect each of these guys in their own way, although the real joys that I shared with Davy were special. At one point we had some good hard connections, but as the years rolled on, those things faded away. But I am sorry to see Davy go. He was the one member in the group that I had the strongest human connection with. I still have two guys that I love and respect left from the band, but we share a different dynamic.[251]

*

I'm sitting in my hotel room after tonight's show, mulling over the evening's event. Tonight, for the first time, Micky and I went on stage, here at the Fantasy Springs hotel and casino, just the two of us, as The Monkees.

Before virtually every show The Monkees ever did, starting with the very first show we did in Hawaii in 1967, the four of us, or three of us, had a little huddle and said, "Hober reeber sober sokin'," or words to that effect, as a way of affirming we were on a team.

Tonight Micky and I looked at each other, and, since you can't have a huddle with two people, we had a hug, and said, "Hober reeber…" etc. Having a hug instead of a huddle was a bit strange, but Michael didn't want to do any more touring, and we thought there might be demand for The Monkees anyway, and so, nervous and cautious, Micky and I went out, just the two of us, as The Monkees.[252]

*

I would say I was pretty good friends with Micky, and there was a lot of love between me and Davy. I have a lot of respect for Mike Nesmith and we've structured ways to work together. Things rotate. It's like having a basketball team. You know, gosh, it's like having a championship basketball team. They go on the road every so often and do tours, you know, just exhibition tours but fortunately your music skills don't deteriorate as fast as your basketball skills do, but I wouldn't know what else to compare it to. We had a chance to go out together and we took it, and we had a great time, and if we were not friends at all we would not have been able to do it. We played tours months and months long: '86, '87, '89, '91, '92, '96, '97, 2001, 2002 and 2011, so we couldn't have been such enemies.[253]

*

I can tell you for myself that I liked and respected and loved each of them in different ratios. Although we've looked at the question a number of times amongst ourselves since then, and really it's much more like a championship basketball team getting together for reunions, or the guys at the office, you know? Or it's like, how many people at the place where you work do you think of as family, you know? Some of them. And not all of them. And it's pretty much just that way. We were actors after all — when the scene called for us to be taking care of each other, we did that scene.

I have to say I have a lot of affection for those guys though. Like I said, in different ratios. Hehehe.[254]

*

I learned a lot from and through The Monkees and I wouldn't have traded it for the world in terms of life and experience and so on. But if I had *not* been a member of The Monkees, my feeling is that I *would* have become a popular performer in my own right, because that's what I do, and I would have just kept right on doing it.[255]

*

I don't want to have The Monkees on my back. But I don't have to close the door on my past anymore. I don't have to try to escape from what I've done and been. Everything I am now is a product of all of what I was, and I'm not given to know the whys and wherefores of things as I go through them. Mostly I find out the whys and wherefores afterward.[256]

*

I've sung Monkees songs all my life. I had almost forgotten how [to sing other songs]. I have never sung anything else in thirty years. In the shower, I sing nothing but Monkees songs. The same songs over and over. I sing all the parts. That's all I ever sing.[257]

*

Music has been a strong part of my life. That's why I get so upset when I hear people talk about The Monkees not being able to play instruments. None of us — and I'm talking about [Micky] Dolenz, Mike Nesmith, Davy Jones and myself — were non-musical. We were real musicians and we played real music.

There was a lot of commercial hype involved with the emergence of The Monkees. Without at least a dollop of commercialism, you can't make it in the business. Talent and commercialism go together. People liked to put us down, but we were there and we will be remembered.[258]

*

No matter what happens — and I know this can't go on forever — I will always be one of The Monkees. Each of us will be that. Mike Nesmith, producer of records; Micky Dolenz, TV actor; Davy Jones on Broadway; Peter Tork, folk singer and soloist — we will share having been Monkees together for the rest of our lives.[259]

Tork About Music

Learning to play musical instruments always came easy to me. Other things I couldn't learn no matter how hard I studied.[260]

*

I took piano for five or six years, and then studied theory in college. French horn in high school and college later on. Guitar came next, and the five string banjo came after that. If you play guitar, and particularly if you play Travis picking, you're used to playing bass parts with your thumb, and the strings on a bass are the same as the bottom four strings on a guitar, so if you play guitar, and you pay attention to your bass notes, you can play bass. So I just picked up the bass, that was easy, nothing to it, and I've enjoyed playing bass through the years.

But I'll tell you something, in my view, one of the things about my being an alcoholic is that it did keep me from applying the kind of concentration that let me be as good a musician as I want to be. In other words, it's like every so often I would pick up a new instrument, and so if I could only play a few instruments and play them all commensurately better, I think I'd be a happier musician today.

I really would rather concentrate on the things I can do somewhat well rather than waste time doing things I can't do at all well. So I'm beginning to learn a little bit.[261]

*

When I was about 14 I asked for a banjo, and my folks went out and bought me a little tiny, dinky five-string banjo. And Pete Seeger's book, *How To Play the Five-String Banjo*, I think I bought that myself, and learned how to play from that. Nobody said, "Here, take a banjo," or, "Gee, you'd be good at it," or anything like that. I just wanted to play it.262

*

It was an aluminum Ode long neck with a solid, arched top. I love that banjo — there's nothing like it today. It picks better than any frailing banjo, and it frails better than any picking banjo I've ever heard. You can't replace it. I had to borrow $125 from my grandma to buy it, and I've had it for more than 55 years now.263

*

Very interesting use of the banjo on that cut ["You Told Me"]. I thought it really kicked. My friends all said, "That's your axe, buddy." It really kills when the banjo comes right in the middle and then the band hits with that nice bass drop. That moment is really exciting, that's what music is supposed to be.264

*

I used the Gretsch bass on screen because The Monkees had a deal. I used the solid-body because I didn't like the tone of the Gretsch. Honestly enough, I don't believe the Gretsch had feedback problems in concert, but it sounded muffled to me.265

*

No, I don't still have any of the Gretsch basses that I used. No, I don't still have that Guild bass. No, I didn't catch any flak for using the Guild, and I didn't play much bass on *Headquarters*. Mostly I played keyboards; Chip Douglas played bass for most of the cuts. I believe he used my Guild, though, and I surely did on "You Just May Be the One." I didn't own the Vox organ I played on the show, but they let us keep the Vox amps we played through, though they disappeared pretty quickly, too.

The acoustic guitar I played for the most part was (and still is, thank goodness) my Guild F-30. I got it in '67 while The Monkees were on the road in Nashville. I had just lost a pre-Gibson Epiphone acoustic, about the size of a Guild F-50, stolen! What a loss that was. (That may be the guitar you saw on the show.) But I'd had an F-30 before, and liked it hugely, so that's what I got then. I still have it, and it's the sweetest guitar I know, just about. I'd love to have hung onto that Epiphone, BUT! Oh, well, such is life.[266]

*

For me, the glory was getting to hang with Little Richard for however long, even for just a little bit [on *33 1/3 Revolutions Per Monkee*].

Little Richard said, "You should get out of here… This kid's got it. This kid's into the blues. He's got Rock 'n' Roll in him. He should *be* something."

I haven't quit trying.[267]

*

I can just sit back and enjoy music when it's done as skillfully as it needs to be, and when I get some emotion from it. If I hear problems technically, or I don't believe I hear emotion (and the music does not have to be complicated; simple folk songs are wonderful if done well and with heart), I sit up and begin to parse it out; how would I do it better (if I think I could), etc. Incidentally, I find that because I deal with music with both sides of the brain, as I think all musicians do, I can not have music in the background and carry on a conversation; I'm focused on the music in almost every case.[268]

*

As far as I'm concerned, no instrument is harder than any other, overall. [If you want to] play the banjo, play the banjo. I recommend most particularly Pete Seeger's book, *How to Play the 5-String Banjo.* It was hugely valuable to my learning. The thing about the banjo, at least the way I play it, is that there is a kind of hump that's a bit high getting over right at the start. Once that's behind you (and it'll take a month or six weeks depending on how hard you work at it), the rest of it's a piece of cake.

Incidentally, I reject the notion that anyone doesn't have musical ability. It's true that some learn faster than others, but that's true of everything, and why people should discourage themselves in the musical realm is pretty much beyond me. True musical inability is about as common as congenital blindness. Everyone else can improve with effort. Remember, the surest predictor of success in any endeavor is not talent, but *work*.[269]

*

As to the guitar, your only hope is practice. Firstly, practice the "clamp." That is, you must learn to bring all your fingers down on the neck of the guitar in whatever chord you're playing all at once. None of that, "Ok, the first finger goes here… then there goes the second finger…" No. If you do that, you'll never get anywhere. All the fingers go down at the same time. Practice that. Practice it in the car on an imaginary guitar. Practice it in a way that nobody can see you when you're at the dinner table. Like that.

As to your "deformed" finger, you have no choice, do you, short of surgery. If you keep playing, your finger will become a part of your musicianship, and it will be no more than an idle curiosity. Jerry Garcia and Django Reinhardt both had missing finger joints, and they played pretty well regardless.

Practice against a metronome, and set it as slowly as you need to to begin to make the changes in time. Practice makes perfect, they say, but only if you practice well. If you practice putting your fingers down one at a time, that's what you'll get good at. See?[270]

*

I'm sorry, but I don't believe I can explain an 11th chord to you easily. I didn't know anything about them myself until I'd been playing music for about 15 years. Basically, though, a simple chord consists of the 1st, 3rd and 5th notes of a scale, all played together. If you then add the 7th note to that chord, it's called a 7th chord, and so on up the line. It gets tricky when you get up over the octave because the notes start to repeat, but believe me, it does make sense… eventually. *Smile*[271]

Most performers can get over [stage fright], and it gets easier with practice, but the initial hurdle is a biggie. I will report to you that at the first show I ever did on a stage in front of a paying audience, my knees were actually knocking together. I thought that was just some tired old cliché, but it was what happened. I can also tell you, however, that it's easier on stage than in front of friends and family, often. You may have good results by finding places where you can perform more or less anonymously, at amateur shows, school talent shows, etc.

But here's the main thing, I think. If you want to be a performer, it's a hump you'll have to get over. Take my word for it, what starts out as stage fright becomes a friend of yours as you get into the business of performing. I hope you go for it; we need lots of good young performers if we're going to get through this next several years.

Oh, yeah, almost forgot, very important: practice your craft. Make sure you are comfortable doing what you do before you take it on stage. Practice a lot, make it feel easy to yourself. Make it easy on yourself.[272]

*

Well, it does seem to me that the music to commerce connection is getting worse in some ways, though the Internet seems to be a force in the other direction. I am sure, however, that art and commerce have always, always been uneasy bedfellows. At some level, the artist has had to find a way to glean a few ducats from everybody s/he entertains since the beginning of time, though perhaps in older days fewer of the entertainers did it as a full-time occupation. I believe they more commonly entertained each other when the work was done.

What I believe you're talking about, not limited to the entertainment field, is the seeming growing power of corporate control. The problem here is that corporations are only slightly beholden to the will of the people at large, and they seem to have a life of their own, unchecked by considerations for the well-being of the population beyond their stockholders (most of whom are themselves other corporations). This is very dangerous, I do believe, and it requires enormous vigilance on the part of the rest of us to keep them from going overboard in their materialistic single-mindedness.

Keep asking these questions; they're some of the most important ones confronting society today.[273]

*

A career takes dedication on the part of many different people. One needs people to believe in one, and I cannot muster a career on my own hoof. I don't have what it takes to book shows, make arrangements, and tend to all the details, so it takes a village basically.

But in terms of staying personally balanced in the midst of showbiz requires a particular little extra something — the ability to rely on something or someone or some process that I'm included in. In other words, it's not me and everything else, but a process that I'm included in and can rely upon. Sometimes this works mechanically and sometimes it's transcendent; but it's got to be greater than my solo self, and I need to have something on my side — friends who have insight and a collection of people that I can turn to for spiritual uplifting or a joke here or there. Nobody does this alone, but that's true about everything as far as I'm concerned.[274]

*

I always wanted to be a performer, and I like music a great deal. I'd rather be a musical performer than a comedy performer, but I would rather be a comedy performer than play music all alone, by myself, and never play for anybody else.

I mean, music is about communication anyway, you can hardly be a musician without performing, but I'd rather perform than not. I'd rather play music than do comedy and act. Just basically because I think the ratio of effort to satisfaction is better for me in music.[275]

*

I love music. The craft of it remains endlessly fascinating to me. There isn't much that I want to do other than music. I love a good joke. I love to laugh. Humor is an important part of music.

I don't know how serious a musician I am. I think it actually gives me some grounds for self examination. Sometimes I think that I am an entertainer who uses music to entertain and that I'm not really a good musician. Sometimes I think I'm a really good musician who just uses music. I can never really settle this in my own mind.[276]

*

A few years ago, I met a professional classical piano player by the name of Jeffrey Biegel. We had an enjoyable conversation about classical music and kept in touch thereafter. He later wrote and asked if I would write something for piano and orchestra to be played at an engagement he had with Orchestra Kentucky, an orchestra centered in Bowling Green, KY.

At first I declined, thinking I could never do anything serious like that, at least not without writing obvious stuff. But some ideas began to roll around in my head, and I sat down to play them on the keyboard with the computer catching what I was doing. Lo and behold, strange stuff I liked emerged. What I've put up is the actual performance by Orchestra Kentucky, with Jeffrey Biegel at the piano, recorded January 26th, 2015, at the Southern Kentucky Performing Arts Center.

There's a sculpture outside St. John the Divine cathedral in New York City. It's the symbol for the sun, you know, a disk with little wavy rays coming off it. Only instead of every other ray, there were animals, like a wave then a giraffe and a wave and a hippopotamus. Like that. That helped me to see that the era of the abstract was over, that what was replacing it was traditional images juxtaposed in strange and interesting new ways. That in turn gave me permission to use the kinds of music I knew how to write, only mixing and (mis)matching the various parts.

So that's what I did. I named the piece "moderato ma non troppo." If you ever took music lessons, you know that an awful lot musical direction is in Italian, so I gave my piece a name which in Italian means "moderately, but not too much." Sort of like having your steak cooked medium but not very.

I did use some abstract stuff, but I hope not too much for your enjoyment.

I never thought I'd do something like this, and it was a tremendous thrill to hear what I'd written performed by about 65 musicians… all at once!

I hope you enjoy it. If not, blot it from your memory and we'll never speak of it again. If you do, tell your local orchestra that they very much want to play this piece.[277]

To listen to Peter's Concerto please visit petertork dot bandcamp dot com

*

When you have enough of an awareness of what you're doing, what basketball players call "in the zone", and secure enough with the guys around you that you relax and let the music play you. I'll tell you a secret, the secret is to play within yourself. If you know only four or five notes, play those notes with conviction. The zone is not dependent on your technical ability. If you want to find the zone, find a couple of other guys who play those same notes or like those notes; you'll find it, it'll hit you. You will fall in love with yourself.[278]

*

I tell you, every time SSB gets up on stage and plays, I get off. I get taken away, I get transported, something happens. Maybe not for very long, maybe not very much, I get carried away every night, to some extent or another.[279]

*

There are no particular awards I would like. You know, Oscars, and Grammys and Emmys, those things are fine but I'm not playing the games, and you can't win if you don't play, so I don't know about anything — maybe a Grammy if the record was really fabulous and went places. But that's just incidental, the real rewards are just to be able to play music. That's it. Just allow me to play music in front of some people that might enjoy it and I'm a happy camper. That's all I ever needed.[280]

*

I've been happy to be in group, after group, after group. It's been wonderful. It's been a great ride now that I think of it. It's been a great ride.[281]

Tork About Parenthood

As to your 16-year-old, well, remember that he's at an age where (he thinks) you're responsible for everything that's wrong with his life. It's a function of his age… but 16-year-old kids have been blaming their parents at the best of times. Treat him with dignity and rigorous correctness when at all possible. You'd likely be in for a hard time with him at the best of times, I am sorry to say.

Mainly, however, do not give up hope for a better life all around. There's no telling what may happen, and the single most important thing in your arsenal is to remain as calm as possible, keep doing every sober thing you can think of to make it right, and remember that time wounds all heels. That's a joke, but it's true. If you stay true to what you believe is right, and don't act out rashly or in a mean-spirited or vengeful way, the situation will turn around in the long run. On the other hand, if you do act out from a revenge place, you will likely ruin any chance you may have for a happier outcome. Please ask your friends and, if you have any, spiritual resources for all the help they'll give you.[282]

*

Of course some parents find it easier to kick out their kids than others. That's just natural. But as to the general average of kids today staying more with their parents than in days of yore, well, I partly blame those who let the economy go to hell in a hand basket… or perhaps actively took it there, is a better description.

It's tougher now than it used to be to find a job, and there is less of a spirit that finding one will give one a real chance to come up in the world. It's therefore understandable that 25-year-olds, and some even well older, would be discouraged, and have very little incentive to go forth and make their way. Still, I am pretty sure that wanting to work rather than lay about is a preference in human nature, as long as no major roadblocks stand in the way.

As to whether it was our hippie lifestyle that led us to treat our kids in ways that made them lazy, well, I wouldn't know for sure. But I do know that every generation is formed by the previous generation's reactions to their parents' generation, etc., etc., since time immemorial. We did the best we could with what we had, and if we don't like what we see, I'm not sure we can do much for the next generation anymore.

I believe that my kids appreciate that I am still working on my own life, and that gives them encouragement not to give up, whatever else they may think of me. I don't have much to say about the way they live their lives. Of course, they aren't encamped in my basement, either. Meanwhile, I counsel patience and love, of course.[283]

*

For starters, I will report that my kids' mom and I never *told* them to be polite. Because we were polite to them, they naturally said "please" and "thank you" without any extra prompting on our parts. As to broccoli, well, three-year-olds cannot be expected to be tactful, and whether they eat it or not must be a matter of negotiation, not of coercion, I'm sure. I used to gag at the taste of Brussels sprouts, and nothing could get me to eat them. I still don't like them much.[284]

*

Hallie and Ivan go to an alternative school locally. We decided on it because it's a place where if the kids wanted to do something they can insist on it. My kids have whale watching classes where they rent a boat and go and watch whales. I have never seen it, but they tell me it is a transcendental experience.[285]

*

No, actually, I'm *not* a very good [dad]. No, not as a good as I want to be.

But then, I don't know any dad who *is*, so…[286]

*

Yes I do [have a good relationship with my kids]. My daughter tells me that she has a better relationship with me than any of her friends have with their fathers.

I hope the others aren't catastrophic… because otherwise it's small praise! Yeah, we're doing fine. It's wonderful.[287]

*

It was a tough time [after the cancer surgery] but my daughter, Hallie, 41, was a real support to me.[288]

*

The damage I did do, I have only the vaguest ways of assessing, I have no way of knowing for sure.

I know that my daughter has a terrible time with relationships, and for a long time was involved with one alcoholic after another. I don't want to say that's exactly the damage I caused, but there certainly is a connection between who I was when she was growing up and who she is now.

My enormously talented son won't practice his craft. He's closed in on himself. He's a great guy, and there's lots of ways in which he's okay just the same, but I see that he's cramped in his soul. And I know that that comes from the ways that I treated him, and his mother, when he was growing up.

My best efforts at amends in those cases — after doing my best to sort things out in practical terms — the best I know how to do is to remain as sober as I can, and to grow, and become as expansive in my own life as possible.

If I was a bad example to him as a kid, I hope that I can be a better example to him as he's growing up, as he is now, a young man.[289]

Tork About Peace

My idea of serenity? Knowing that it's okay that things *aren't* okay.[290]

*

If people were more honest and loving, there wouldn't be wars and hate and all the rest of the things that make so many lives tragic and unhappy.[291]

*

Maybe if I let you in on something that worked for me when I had this problem it will help you, too. I hope so.

You have to think of everything as "bads" and "goods". You're probably giving out a "bad" every time you get a "bad" now, aren't you? Let's think about that. What's going to happen?

First of all, you're letting the "bads" take over. If you give a "bad" for every "bad" then pretty soon *everything* will be "bads" and there won't be any room for "goods".

But if you give a "good" for a "bad", no matter how hard it is to do, then you'll find that gradually the "goods" will take over. You'll find that things will be super-groovy in a while.

Let me know how it works out.[292]

*

Y ou make me blush with shame, actually. I suppose I am a lot better at that calm, sage-like thing than I ever was before, but it's a far cry from where I'd like to be with it.

What does work for me is to realize that I have resources whom I may call on; with that comes the patience to wait until it's appropriate that I reach out. That is to say, if, say, I were in your shoes, I might not be able to drop everything and call my best spiritual brother or sister, but knowing that I'll be able to *after* my shift is over gives me the patience to not act out... sometimes! Heheheh.

I have gained a great deal from knowing that whatever's going on around me, it *isn't about me*. This one has taken time, and I'm a bit slow to remember this when challenged, but I get around to it eventually, and when I get there, nothing anybody does pushes my buttons any longer. My buttons are a part of my early life, and I strive to remember that what's happening in the here and now is not how things used to be, even if they remind me of those times in very vivid ways.

I repeat, however, that I'm a far cry from any consistency on this matter; I only claim to be getting better at it. It's way too slow a process for me, and for some of my friends, too, I imagine, but it's as fast as I can go, and I just have to make what peace with it I may.[293]

*

I am not one of those who believes that everything is for the best. The only thing I'm sure of is that I can bring the best attitude possible to the situation. It seems to me that you believe you had a bargain with the forces of Karma, and that you feel betrayed. Betrayal is very infuriating, to be sure, but the laws of God and/or Karma are not actually known to us, merely guessed at. I've learned recently to ask myself one question: *Would you rather be right, or happy?*

I urge you to let go of what you thought was your due, and find the best way to live with what you got. There's still a lot of joy to be had regardless, I am sure.[294]

*

There's a social revolution going on and the young ones are into it. The young more automatically agree to change. When they grow up, they'll be just as anti-revolutionary as their parents, but about different things. If you want something really visionary and mystic, telepathy is the coming phenomenon. Nonverbal, extrasensory communication is at hand. Love.

I don't mean it to sound corny. Dogmatism is leaving the scene. Youth is examining all the old-time premises that used to be taken totally for granted — sexual mores, artistic mores. And in Russia, the revolutionary clichés. I think there's a genuinely democratic society just over the horizon. I hope so. I hope it achieves freedom and peace.

Draft status? 1-Y. Unacceptable. I don't like the army, and the army and I came to an agreement. To put it bluntly, they thought I was crazy… and maybe I am.

I don't think I'm less patriotic than anyone else, maybe I'm even more. I think you should stand for what you believe in. I stand for love and peace. To my way of thinking, they're the same thing. But the man who said, "My country, right or wrong," made a slight error of judgement. My country wrong needs my help. Well, I guess I've got myself in enough hot water.[295]

*

I believe very much in all that I believed in back in the 60's. I hope I'm more aware of the practicalities than I was then, but I am positive that the values and principles I held then are critical to the well-being of the planet, or at the very least, critical to growth and contentment in the population.

As to the practicalities: the chance of no more war in our lifetimes is so close to zero that I don't imagine it possible, though there well may be progress along these lines. Maybe. Sometimes I see the world as an eternal horse race between salvation and dissolution, now one, and now the other gaining the lead.

But to the extent that we can learn, each and all of us, that the cooperative good is good for the greatest individual good (with safeguards, to be sure), that forgiveness is the route to true inner peace, and that not everything we deem wrong or bad may be so, to that extent hassles of all shapes, sizes and colors will diminish.

Would, I hope, be willing to bet my life on these principles.[296]

*

Firstly, I grieve for those who lost their lives and loved ones on 9/11. Further, it is my hope that the memories of this day will inspire us all to sympathy and understanding, not only for the direct victims of the 9/11 attack and its aftermath, but for all who suffer and have suffered from aggression, injustice and oppression.[297]

*

On September 11, I was in the Chicago area, and I was about to fly home to L.A. I saw some pictures of the collapse of a radio tower as I was glancing at a T.V. screen, but didn't think much of it for a few minutes. It took maybe 15 minutes for the proportions of the event to dawn on me. I wound up driving home in the car I'd rented for traveling around Chicago. By chance, my then-bandmate Tadg Galleran was also in Chicago, and wanted to get home, too. It took us just about 48 hours to get home.

While I'm on the subject, though, and I know you didn't ask, I'd like to say one thing about 9/11. A lot of scorn and abuse has been heaped on those who suggest that this country may have had a part in the events of that day. I personally find the idea that we (as a country) never did anything bad to anybody else, and that the only reason anyone would do anything to us is their unbridled inhuman evil, to be very far wide of the truth. The number of times I have been accosted in one way or another where I had nothing to do with it is maybe in the 3-5% range, if that. I'm not excusing anyone from blame. But the more we think we're all good and certain *others* are all evil, the worse things get, not the better they get. Only the humility to realize *my* part in the events of my life allows me to walk in relative peace. The other attitude is called pride, in the seven-deadly-sins sense of the word, and the Bible is dead right when it says it goes before a fall.

Hope this isn't too disturbing.[298]

*

At what times do you feel that there's hope for the human race?

All the time. Are you kidding? What's the alternative?[299]

Tork About Peter Thorkelson

I think I am [a pretty sharp cookie], and not to put any false modesty, but the truth is — about my not thinking about [or being concerned about] the publishing [rights to my songs] — is actually a character trait that I've come to recognize as being a character trait that contributed to my character. The Peter Tork character on the TV show was not only a little simpler than I am, but also blithe and unconcerned, and that *is* me. I mean I didn't even know this about my life. Performers create their characters out of themselves, out of something that they wish they were, or something they secretly believe they are but can't ever actually be in public. John Wayne, he created that character because it's what he wanted to be. People create characters out of themselves. It's not like that guy I created was a totally different character, we have a lot in common, him and me.[300]

*

When I was 16, I just didn't have any confidence in myself. I really thought I was devoid of any kind of sex appeal. But today all of that is really changing.

It used to be that the girls I dated weren't necessarily beauties, but now it seems they're getting more and more beautiful because I have added confidence in myself as a person.

Now by beauty, I don't necessarily mean what's on the outside. I mean the whole of a person. Her mind, her soul, and her body. In other words, the total person. A more complete person is a more beautiful person.

I thought a lot of things about myself when I was younger that just weren't true. Now that I'm older and I have studied I think I'm beginning to understand where it's at. Before I just didn't. Now I can forget myself and enjoy what I'm doing because I'm not really searching to find out who I am anymore. I know.

I had no faith [when I was 16]. I was constantly leaning on other people. This wasn't fair to them or to myself.[301]

*

As a matter of fact, the interesting thing is that ["Tork"] came about because, in my Greenwich Village days, I was wearing my father's high school sweatshirt, and it said "Tork" on the back of it because it was *his* nickname.

Thorkelson got shortened that way, and for a long time, I wasn't even Peter Tork, I was just Tork. And some of my friends from back then still just call me Tork as though it were my first name, which is kind of funny.[302]

*

I'm bothered by people who regard me as a star rather than just a regular fellow.[303]

*

Barbara sees me as a mixed bag, but basically worth it.[304]

*

Some of you keep writing and asking if I've become a complete vegetarian these days. Well, the answer is... nearly, but not quite. Actually I'm following a special Eastern diet, of yin and yang foods. That's right! So you're asking me EXACTLY what it is that I eat. It's things like brown rice, and yoghurt, and special raw milk and drinks like herbal teas. And organically grown vegetables and fruits. I'm feeling great on it. Who knows, I might end up a dietician one of these days...[305]

*

I don't eat pizza, generally. No, don't eat pizza. Don't eat tomatoes. Don't eat cheese. I don't eat cheese for the throat, you know, 'cos you can't sing with cheese...

Davy Jones:

Did you ever try swallowing it? If you swallow it, you'll be able to sing.[306]

*

One thing I have discovered in recent years is that I suffer from Asperger's syndrome — a form of autism. There is a fanaticism and obsessiveness about me and my actions that appear to bear this out.[307]

*

The characteristic I most dislike in myself is my lack of concentration. Some have called me ADD. My sister thinks I have ADD, and uh... by the way, you want to go riding on a bike?[308]

*

I grew up believing that I had nothing to say, that nobody was interested in anything that I had to say. It took me a long time to get over that and through that. Even now there's probably some of that left. My sense of overdoing it on the speaking thing: I carry on speaking and sometimes I feel like I'm straining at the bit to get these things said.[309]

*

Why can't a modest person be a perfectionist? Everything I do must be done well.[310]

*

I look up and see that this is my life. My only serious acquired skill is that of an entertainer. I did disassociate myself for many years because of a misplaced idealism. I was buying all that stuff about The Monkees not being musicians or real human beings. Back then I was entirely too malleable. I now do not have the remotest idea why I did many of the things I did. In recent times I have had to grunt, groan and strain to become a genuine businessman and take control of my career. The ultimate responsibility lies with me and I have recently agreed with God to do it, however poorly. That is the change in me.[311]

*

To the outside observer, I'm sure it looked as though I had succumbed to the extremities of a given culture. To me, I simply exhibited moderate good sense. Basically, I lived at a poverty level, scratching for odd jobs. I wore a beard, my hair was past my shoulders, and I was working in a restaurant, singing folk songs and waiting tables. I was playing piano and was in and out of various rock groups. I played lead guitar for a rock group called Osceola. No records. I was in the bass section of the Fairfax Street Choir, a thirty-five member vocal group. I also fronted a group of my own and tried to make a demo, but it didn't go anywhere. I had a job offer to come out here to Venice. I also worked as a high school teacher.

The mass media has a tendency to distort. As long as capitalism remains the underpinning of society, what is good will always take a back seat to what will sell. General Motors isn't concerned with making a quality automobile. Sears isn't concerned with offering a quality television set. All that counts in a capitalistic society is selling. And to the mass media's way of thinking, a picture of Peter Tork as a so-called "burned-out hippie" with a beard and long hair implies a hopeless case who can't lift his hand to his face to get his razor up and who has no interest except in stealing to support his drug habit. If that's what sells, they'll print that. The truth of the matter is, my primary concern was, and is, self-realization in a social setting.[312]

*

I can't give you [the best] individual moments, but I can tell you that getting sober was the most important change in my life ever! I have had a few moments here and there where I was certain that all was in order in the cosmos. Those were wonderful, too.[313]

*

I'm sure that without the ego collapse it took to free me from the clutches of active alcoholism, I would not be alive today. It was, sadly, too long a process, but that it came at all will be my greatest event, no matter what else happens to me.[314]

*

My greatest achievement is escaping the hell and misery of drugs and alcohol. Being human, it's an amazing thing. You know it's not an easy thing, it's a scary business, and having the help and the hope makes it doable. Just being here. Now.[315]

*

The basic thing that keeps me safe and secure is no distractions. As long as nobody is in my face or jumping around, or you know, I'm in any kind of particular danger, I'm pretty safe and secure all the time. I guess I feel a little bit more of that on a massage table.[316]

*

Change everything about me and then ask: Who I am? Well, that's a puzzler.

If you're asking what other fields I've been drawn to, to any noticeable degree, I don't mind saying that the law, and the kind of counseling I do in these columns, have both looked like reasonable and attractive careers. Strangely enough, there's one other thing in particular I wouldn't mind doing, and that's massage therapy. My father had good hands, and he seems to have bequeathed them to me, and though I've never taken training, and it's a little late in life to get started now, it still seems like a useful life to me.[317]

*

If I had any other careers I was thinking of law at one point. And I thought psychotherapy, thought I might be good at that 'cos I've worked so hard on my own sanity![318]

*

If you're asking me what talents I would like to have some of, there are any number of talents, you know?

Tact. I'd love to have tact for a talent, that would be really great.

Consistency. There's a lot of things that I slip and slide around on.

But for the most part I kinda like the hand I got dealt.[319]

*

I'm not exactly sure I can tell you [which career I would choose to do all over again], and therein may lie my greatest problem in life. I wish I played a lot *fewer* instruments a lot *better*. Although I am pretty sure that the actor's life is not for me, and I'm not as qualified to be a teacher (at least in the conventional classroom setting) as I'd like to be. Basically I count myself an entertainer whose medium is mostly music, rather than a musician who entertains. If I had to do it all over again, I believe I'd focus on music.[320]

*

I'm a simple, uncomplicated person. I don't have to go creative just to make a phony image of myself. I just like to play my guitar, and that's all. I love music.[321]

*

The top thing on my lifetime list to is make it as a blues pop musician on my own.[322]

*

Being in a group is about the only thing I've ever really wanted to do, I've wanted to do many, many things in my life, but the most consistent and deepest desire has been to be part of a good musical group.[323]

*

My life is, you know, what's important is stuff that *moves* me. Now, Jimi Hendrix moves to this day, those early records of his move me. I am, I am swept away, I get involved on an artistic basis, I want to join what's going on there on the inside. That, to me, is important.[324]

*

Are you nervous going up on stage? No. I anticipate, I gear myself up, the process of going up on stage involves a lot of mental stuff, which is not nervousness anymore, it's just preparation. My own internal work is about being sure that I feed myself enough, emotionally, psychically, spiritually and so on.[325]

*

The Court Jester [1956], a musical comedy starring Danny Kaye, was one I loved as a kid. It certainly stands up today. It's just one of the greatest film comedies. My wife Pam saw that and said, "Ah, I see where you get all your stuff." She thinks all my comedic, goofy characters are all contained in that movie.[326]

*

I don't know that [fame] affected my ability to have friendships. Basically I don't think I knew how to be, or have, a friend beforehand, and I don't think I learned while I was in that operation. I mean, I had some good buddies, but that wasn't the same thing. I didn't really understand. There was only one person in my life that I could turn to when I was hurting, who happened somehow to know what it was, what it took to stop me hurting, and that was a woman named Karen Harvey, who later joined me on the West Coast. And I thought, well here's a friend come to join me and this will be a *real* friend. And we were pretty good friends, I guess, but I didn't know what a friend did, in the sense of how, on a day to day basis, do you maintain your friendships, do you go out of your way to make sure that things are nice and right — you know, the kind of work that a friendship takes. You don't just have a friendship without work. And I didn't know that. And I'm not so sure I know it now. I can say it, but I don't know if I have the real gut understanding it takes.[327]

*

Twice I've seen colors. Once I was so totally in love that everything was *pink*; I mean, rosy, like that dusty pink that is the rose color. I swear to God, rose-colored glasses, man. It was, I swear to God, it was as if a pair of rose-colored glasses had been implanted in my eyes. Everything had this hue, and it was just, you feel, "Okay!" And then once, I came downstairs, and my parents had had a lot to drink the night before, and the air was *black*. And incidentally, on our last [Shoe Suede Blues] CD, Saved By The Blues, is the song "Saved By The Blues", which contains all this stuff. A friend of mine [Michael Levine], I'd just talked to him the way I'm talking to you, and he went home and wrote a song, and called it "Saved By The Blues."[328]

*

I always believe things will work out. My happy-go-lucky attitude has kept me sane, or at least as sane as I can ever be.[329]

*

As for myself, the most engaging thing a fan ever did was a certain piece of art. I can't describe its appearance, I can only say the effect on me was magical, and I made it a point to become acquainted with the fan in question. We subsequently spent several happy weeks together over the course of a couple of years. Sadly, we no longer communicate, but it was pretty nice while it lasted.[330]

*

I would say my greatest fear was cosmological disintegration and excruciating agony. Nothing much. I don't fear very much.[331]

*

Well, I'll tell you the truth, I actually thought I was [wearing my belt buckle on the side], A, to be weird, beat, and [B], get the belt buckle out of the way of the guitar.

And about, I don't know, maybe ten years ago, somebody said, "Yeah, that's what the bad boys did in high school, right?"

I went, "Oh my god, it's true." I'd forgotten the bad boys did [that] in high school.[332]

*

Long before I got wind of The Monkees project, when I did my laundry, I just throw the socks in a sock drawer without sorting and pairing them. One day I was dressing in a hurry, and finding a matched pair seemed like a waste of time, so I just grabbed two unmatched socks and put them on. Later it occurred to me that matching socks was all very well and good, but I didn't have to be tied to the idea. I still rarely wear matching socks, though, now more often than I used to, I will admit.[333]

*

I wear different colored socks because nothing is the same.[334]

*

The quick answer is, no, at least consciously, I didn't choose orange and purple because of their connection to hindu yoga. I was first drawn to orange by the eye-grabbing combination of the red-orange and blue-range colors. They just soaked my eye. Blue didn't actually grab me by itself, but orange stuck with me. As to the purple tie, I just thought that that was a great color for a band called Shoe Suede Blues. I never actually gave the decision much thought, but what thought there was was just simply as I said.[335]

*

I was doing an interview once and they asked me if there's any last words I wanted to do, and I said, "Be a hero to yourself." And it kind of just popped out of my mouth. But the more I think about it, the more I like it, the more real it becomes to me.

Being a hero to yourself means that one — me, you — is in charge of one's own life. There's so much goes on, people say, "Who do you think you are?" And who I think I am is who I really think I am, and I get to operate from that basis, and not on the basis of what *you* want from me, or what *you* think is better for me to be, or do. I know that what you want from me is important to *you*, but it doesn't constitute an emergency on my part.

I get to be a hero to myself. I recommend it.[336]

*

You know, I always have this closing message that I like to do. It actually came out of my mouth spontaneously at one of these interviews — "Be a hero to yourself." And I kind of, part of me was waiting to be asked, and part of me was surprised to hear it come out. And I later on ended up giving a graduation speech on the topic.

The point being that everybody yells at you from the time you're two — "Share, share, share! What makes you think you're different from anybody else? How dare you take what isn't yours." And kids who are not psychologically ready for that kind of approach are really befuddled. And they grow up in confusion, not knowing that, in fact, you *are* different from everybody else, and you are in charge of yourself, and you are responsible for this thing that is called your life. And you have to be a superhero. You have to have a cape and a blazing symbol on your chest and be in charge of the life that is yours, against all comers. There are evil-doers and there are people who are telling lies and mean well, and people who are telling the truth and don't mean well, and you have to sort it all out for yourself. And there will be help — you can't do without help — this is the other half of the equation: You can't do this without help. Because that's part of the nature of being human.

But you are still the hero. So that's my message.[337]

*

I used to ask myself, "Why me?" before.
Now I'm saying, "What the hell, why not?"[338]

Tork About Prejudice

I hate prejudice and violence. Somehow, those two seem to go hand-on-hand. It's only fear, lies and bad leadership that keeps us all from loving each other and from seeing each other clearly and purely with the eye of the mind and love of the heart. I believe you can tell more about people by the way they look walking away from you than you can by what they say.[339]

*

I HATE prejudice and violence. Somehow, those two seem to go hand-in-hand. Think of it this way: suppose we lived in a country where everybody was green, and then some orange and purple polka-dotted people came along. Soon we would be saying, "Gee, what funny-looking polka-dotted people!" But because people are basically good in their hearts, each group would want to be friendly with the other. It's only fear, lies and bad leadership that keeps us all from loving each other and from seeing each other clearly and purely with the eye of the mind and the love of the heart.[340]

*

There's so much to think about and so much you have to consider before you make decisions. I started to say judgments, but I don't believe that you should judge others. You can only judge as far as your personal opinion goes. There's no other basis on which to judge people, and that's not a particularly good one. How do you know you're right? You can say, "Well it's only my opinion." But you're still judging. Do you see what I mean?"[341]

*

Question to Peter:

My boyfriend and I have been dating seriously for three years, and in that time, have come across more example of discrimination than I would care to recap. We would like to know: what is your opinion on gay rights? Should we be treated with common decency and respect, or are we subhuman because we happen to be in love? Do we not deserve the right to marry, or adopt children? And why do people, who think of themselves as good people, treat other human beings this way?

Answer:

Is this a trick question? Because the answer(s) is (are) the same whether you're gay, black, a woman, Jewish, Catholic, handicapped, poor... have I left anyone out? (And I don't want to hear middle-class straight white males try to tell me that they're discriminated against in this modern, PC world. We m-c, s, w m's are incredibly privileged, and while I'm sorry for the poor schlub who feels his place has been taken by somebody less qualified, etc., I think of the deprivations historically visited on all the above-mentioned before I get too indignant.)

Oh, and one more thing. Everybody, believe it or not, believes that they are good people doing the best they can. There are very few exceptions, and even most of those few exceptions believe that they're only getting back what was rightfully theirs in the first place. The very, very few exceptions left have errors in their brain circuitry that block their learning about such a thing as real, as opposed to public, consequences. These people are called sociopaths, and there seems to be no help for them.

Everybody's scared, you know. Everybody, to some extent or another.

Trembling.[342]

Tork About Politics

I need to communicate, and while that means entertainment now, it probably means politics later on. You see, I have a missionary view about a lot of things going on that I think I might help them fix.

Listen, an entertainer is a citizen, just as much a citizen as the banker or businessman. More so most of the time, if anyone judges by the taxes paid by entertainers. So you tell me if a guy cares about what is going on, and he's been supporting his government for years with a bunch of bucks, why shouldn't he get in there and try to do what he thinks will make things better?

Look, let's say, just for the heck of it, that some joker did just act his way into office, huh? Okay, then what? He's got to produce after he gets there, hasn't he? And that, pal, is where he finds his moment of truth. If he does a lousy job, he won't get elected the second time. You can bet on that. And if he does a good job, why shouldn't he be re-elected, just like a lawyer, or anybody else?

But even so, I still consider myself a happy guy. Basically, I'm an optimist. I believe things are getting better all the time. Maybe not second to second, but year by year. There's a lot to be done, though.

You see, one of these days, I aim to get my help out there. And I really think I can help.[343]

*

They didn't want me criticizing the war right at the outset. Can't think why.

"You don't criticize the president!" they said.

"But, he's *wrong*..."

I didn't push it. I'm not a very activist kind of guy. I'm not. My opinions are very strong, but I don't march and I don't play politics.[344]

*

I never did march. I never did carry a sign. The only thing I did was a sit-down strike someplace once. Not much, I never really did get into activism, and I don't know whether it's just because I'm a flat out coward or because I have some deep understanding of the cosmic truth of the fact that it doesn't do any good, in whatever case, that's what it is, I don't do it much.[345]

*

Sarah Palin was a hoot, and gave the Republicans something to hang their hats on. In my judgment, from a policy and administrative point of view, she was no more qualified to be vice president than an 11-1/2-year-old. She got lots of traction from being "folksy," and for being without doubt. That is a large part of what got W elected. The American people do not want nuance in their elected leaders, at least not at the national level.[346]

*

As to the "[Sarah Palin] phenomenon," I don't worry about that anymore. You can fool some of the people all of the time, and there's no getting over that. The job for the rest of us is simply not to demonize anyone, and to fight as hard as needed for what we are sure is right.

As to what the "young-ish" can do, I propose what I propose the old-timers do: do what's in front of you to do with gusto (you'll never find out how things are if you do them half-assedly), and remember that everyone's doing his or her best, no matter how awful that may be.[347]

Tork About Possessions

Right now my most treasured position is my house. I've recently moved into the house my parents moved us to when I was 13. It's a pre-revolutionary war colonial house in Connecticut, and it is really something to behold.[348]

*

I am a property landlord, making me the object of the revolutionary class. I am also a revolutionary, making me a schizophrenic.[349]

*

My acoustic guitar, that I bought in 1967. I had a guitar stolen, I was in Nashville at the time, and was a fan of what was then being called the F-30 by Guild. And I went to a music store in Nashville, and they had two of them, and I took away the one that I liked better, paid $175 for it. And when you get a guitar that sounds as good as that, you pay $3,500 today, I think, at least. And that is the best, about the best acoustic guitar I've ever played in my life, and it's (chuckles), it's *mine*.[350]

*

The struggle involved in keeping those people who want what you've got from getting it deprives you of the time to really be yourself. Instead of struggling to keep things out of everybody's hands, if you give what you've got – as Jesus said – if you give away what you've got, life unfolds for you [*If you want to be perfect, go, sell what you have and give to the poor, and you will have treasure in heaven; and come, follow Me.* Matthew, 19:21] And the Catholic church would have us believe that heaven doesn't happen until *after* the death of the body. But I report differently. I report that heaven is an experience available in this life. And it comes from giving your shit away. If you give away your heart, your life, your soul, your goods, and live as close to the bone as you can prudently do, and don't worry about next week, if you live as close to that level as possible, you will find yourself as happy as possible. If you put your faith in the *future*, you're going to be chasing something all your life. Put your faith in the *present*; it's all right.[351]

*

I am absolutely of the optimistic believer in the better angels of our nature type of guy, and I absolutely was then. Being that way, you tend to overlook the harder realities. The British have this expression, gobsmacked, which is a great expression — it's like being hit with a big wet fish. As reality hit me, I was gobsmacked at every turn, and years and years later, now, as we're talking, I think I've had my education and I'm not stupid about the way things are, but I still believe in the sunnier angels of our nature. I've just become less sanguine about how we were going to fix the world by tomorrow. That's clearly not going to happen, because too many people have too much of a stake in what's wrong with the world, as far as I'm concerned, and I believe it's all fear. I don't believe anybody, given the full choice — except for sociopaths — would prefer to be operating on a basis of greed and acquisition, because everybody knows that the actual possession of things themselves does not generate any longterm satisfaction. Everybody knows this, and yet people keep chasing the carrot, even though they sort of know that it's tied to their own heads and they'll never get it, they still keep chasing it because they don't know how not to.[352]

*

Look at those of us here, right now. We are incredibly fortunate, we're really very, very lucky. All of us know just to take care of the physical side of things. We all know where we're going to eat next, and where we're going to sleep next, and a lot about who our friends are, and a lot about what we're going to be doing for the next few days, if not weeks, months, and years. And there are people in this world who *don't* have any of that. [In society] it's like, "I'm taking mine, I'm cutting, I don't care what anybody else…"

I don't know where this all came from, but it seems to be happening everywhere. What I think I see is people — they have homes and money, and they think that makes them more human than people who don't.[353]

*

Those of us who came into the public eye did so partly to escape what was awful growing up, be it oppressive households or oppressive social situations. Give us a jolt of acceptance singing or dancing or telling jokes, etc., and we go whole hog for a life of that public acceptance.

Unhappily, though, fame is the same as what we're told about collecting possessions; they satisfy for a bit, but if there isn't some way to make you (myself/one's self) whole, the possessions are only temporary satisfactions at best. When a performer leaves the stage, he/she can't take the public acclaim with her. Drugs are another of those things which distract or divert from, or numb us to, the sadness we still carry within. It's a terrible paradox that those who go beyond the normal boundaries in pursuit of fuller self-expression take chances with their lives beyond the normal boundaries as well.

Meanwhile, there are answers to this problem. They're simple but not easy. The problem may be seen to be that there is no one trustworthy enough to follow. If you grow up like that, it will be very difficult to find reliable guides in this life. There is a True Guide, however. Many follow the God of their understanding. Others are so turned off by religion and all its adherents that nothing under the name of God will serve. That's okay; the True Guide does not have to have the title God to be useful. It does require an understanding of, and a willingness to, pursue whatever in life might usefully lead us to an acceptance greater than the temporary one provided by acclaim or possessions.

The understanding of this greater acceptance will come slowly, but it comes to those who are willing to keep open their eyes and minds.[354]

*

If you hook your life to any material thing, it's going to take you up, but it's eventually going to take you down. You have to hook your life to spiritual values, 'cos that's the only thing that can continue to take you *up* indefinitely.[355]

Tork About Purpose

How do you (or how does anybody) know what to do in life? Someone once said to me, if you don't know what to do, it's because you don't know who you are.

See, for me, I never realized out loud, so to speak, that music/entertainment was my calling. But I look back on my life, and at every juncture, that's what I went for. So, one way of looking at what you might want to do/be in life is to look *back* at what you've liked to do so far.

One note in particular at this point, which I've made before: Everybody gets shut down to some extent growing up; it's inevitable, and nothing to get bent about. But what it does mean is that it's possible that you haven't thought about the things you liked to do as a child for a long time now. Go back into your past. What turned you on? What gave you the thought: I'd like to do that/be a part of that? Even if it was the way you related to your dolls, there might well be a clue there, if not even an outright signpost with a fanfare.[356]

*

Should? I don't know from *should* anymore. I once heard someone say, "Don't 'should' on yourself." I eventually worked it out to where the word "should" requires the phrase "in order to." You "should" turn left here "in order to" get to the grocery store. Like that. So, the question becomes, "in order to"… *what*?

Do you know what you want to be when you grow up? No? Well, perhaps a little investigation is in order. When you were little, what did you dream of becoming? Airline pilot? Doctor, nurse, veterinarian or horse trainer? Wonder Woman? Rock star?

Newspaper reporter? Or did you imagine that a life of marriage and kids plus a bit of a trade as, say, a hair stylist was heaven on earth? Go back to your early daydreams and see whether any of them still holds a charge. Be careful here: if you don't know instantly what your dreams were, then it's possible that you were discouraged from holding on to them. If that's true, then that discouragement will get in the way of your trying to access those dreams now. Be extremely gentle with yourself, even to the point of sickeningly coddling yourself (for a little while anyway, heheheh).

If your childhood dream comes to the fore, you will have all you need to decide whether and where to go to college, or whatever else you may need. One note: it's wonderful to decide to, say, become a musician, but if "famous musician" is your goal, you may be in for more trouble than you want. If you pursue your dream for what it gives you, and let it take you where it will, you will have a pretty cool life almost, no matter what. I'm really sure about this.[357]

*

What writers I know of say is, if you want to be a writer, you're probably not going to do very well. If you must write, then *write*! Do you see the difference? Rainer Maria Rilke wrote *Letters to a Young Poet,* which I recommend on this point. (It's a small book, and cheap at the bookstore, and free at your library.)

I was in my 50's before I put together the notion that A) I should/could select a career, and B) the observation of what it was I did and liked to do.

I've been an entertainer since I was 15, and I never thought of it as a *career choice* 'til vastly later. Perhaps you'll come to an understanding of yourself that includes a selection of a trade, much earlier than I did. I hope you do.

BTW, day job, shmay job. When you need money, you'll do what you have to, be it x-ray tech, or macburgerslinger. Remember to consider what you can *bring* to the situation, rather than concentrating on what the job is going to *suck out* of you. You might also check out your lifestyle, to see if you've gotten yourself more involved with the material world than would allow you to do what you want.[358]

*

I never experienced a fork in the road until my forties. When I first started off, I remember being an entertainer at four, I remember being self-aware as an entertainer at four. I didn't actually think that I was going to *be* an entertainer, I just became one through the course of events; I was in Greenwich Village and they were playing on the coffee houses and I picked up my banjo and went and played and that was all I knew. I didn't have any sense of, "I'll be an entertainer, I'll play music." I just did it, and I thought that I was letting my life lead me on.

Finally when I was 40, I went, "I could make a choice and become *dedicated*." I didn't become dedicated 'til then. A lot of entertainers will tell you that. They didn't become dedicated until much later.[359]

*

Actually what I have found is that often [when creating], things come to me out of the blue, little bits and pieces. When I'm determined to write something then I sit down and do nothing else, and when I do nothing else then the bits and pieces tend to focus in on my project, whatever I'm doing.

Sometimes I'll ruminate and something will come in out of the left field, and I won't be able to use it except put it down for further reference, but when I'm sitting down just working on a particular project it turns out that it is very much like any kind of work — if you just keep at it, the things you need come to you.

I don't think that there's as much difference between the creative process and mundane work as everybody else does. I think that there's much more creativity to normal work and there's much more grind to the creative work than anybody believes. And if you're going to be creative you'd better be willing to sit down, you know, for if not eight hours then six, and if not six then four, and if not five days a week then four, but you'd better find some way to do it *regularly* and be willing to sit with it, and sit *still* with it, and do nothing else.

My tendency is always to get up and divert, you know, I sit down and get so antsy sometimes that I *can't* sit still, and I have to get up and make a cup of coffee, watch television or eat chocolate or chase women or something... pick up my guitar or I don't know what else.

So it is a matter of rigor, of doing it, and what I find is, that generally speaking, inspiration comes, it is not even inspiration, it is, you know, the *tools* you need to do the work.[360]

*

What had gotten me out of organized show business in the first place were the tensions involved with having to deal with power-hungry people.

I thought: "If this is what show business is like, I don't want to have any part of it."

Then, when I worked at this highly autocratic school, I found exactly the same things going on. It was at that point that I finally decided to make my push for show business again. I thought, I might as well do what I like to do, where there's a chance for the big bucks. Even if I don't have them, at least I'll be doing what I enjoy.[361]

*

It's never too late. Of course, there are practical considerations: paying the rent and other bills, eating… like that. If you want to do anything along any lines at all, you must start by arranging your life to give you the time you need, like taking a smaller living space, etc., then you must give all the time you have to doing what it is you want to do.

Do you have an instrument? Get one. Are there theater groups near you? Go to one and (sorry, but this is how they usually start you off) build sets and help in any other way possible. I truly believe that just about your only chance is in complete immersion. Give it everything you've got.[362]

*

Many folks make New Year's resolutions, and there's never a bad time to make decisions to move up in the world or in the heart. And yet I hope and expect that you and I hold a constant desire to do better in the community, personal, and spiritual worlds.

Still, this pause between the last holiday of the year and the celebration of the new year coming in can be a very good time for the kind of contemplation that leads us onward and upward.

Whether you are a devout follower of a religion or one whose only spiritual belief is in the light as a symbol of growth (and, incidentally, the beginning of the return of longer days), I can say for us all: Lead, Kindly Light.[363]

*

Almost without exception, every show I do, I get that *this* is what I'm here for.³⁶⁴

Tork About Regret

Well, as to: did I ever do anything I really regret? The answer is yes and no... sort of.

Of course there are things I did which I recognize turned me away from where I thought I wanted to go. BUT, I find that in just about every case, I needed to go through what happened to find out what I didn't know. In other words, if nothing bad had happened, I wouldn't have had the information to know I'd made a mistake. If you ever could have driven home drunk, you were going to get a DUI sooner or later. Now's as good a time as any.[365]

*

Biggest regret?

Many of the things I failed to follow through on. The fact that I have this history.[366]

*

I don't know if I can handle that question because I would have to use present day awareness to my past misfortunes. I know I wouldn't drink as heavily as I did, that would have made a difference. There are a number of things I would do different. I had a lot of early adventures and sometimes I was just grasping at things out of fear. Sometimes, not knowing what to do, you run like hell to keep up, or at least you think that way. I think I would have taken my time and been a more faithful person.[367]

*

Then I started accumulating a household, and the household was too big for the [Rogerton Drive] house... We moved out of that and into the big house, which is a disastrous move, and one of the worst mistakes I ever made. That was the Wally Cox house. That was a terrible mistake, it turns out. The one mistake I would like to have altered is to have remained at that little house all the time. I'd probably be there still.[368]

*

I cannot imagine wanting to change the smallest particle. Not that it's all been pleasant, by any stretch, but I clearly needed every bump on the road, and bump on the head, to have what I have now, and I wouldn't want to give up a thing, thank you very much. Thank you very much.[369]

*

Any regrets? None. There are lots of things that I wish that I had done differently but if I hadn't done them wrong I wouldn't know what was right. So no regrets, it's all been a learning experience.[370]

Tork About Relationships

Why did you get together with somebody? You look back on your relationship and wonder, "Oh, what the heck, what the heck!" Happily, we produced a daughter, who is a great joy and a pleasure to me, and if I had no other reason for being with this woman of repute, this would have been enough. On the other hand, the personal relationship between us sucked. But she was a good looker. You see, the thing was, at that time of my life I was very shallow. I couldn't see beneath the surface.[371]

*

I lived three years with a picture-pretty woman, and it wasn't very satisfying. It was all right, I don't want to put Reine down just cause she's picture-pretty, but it's better with a woman who is not picture-pretty — in that classic, old photoplay-movie star thing that's going on — and have brains. I'd rather they had brains and character.[372]

*

You might not ever really know whether to stay or not. There are always things tugging us in different directions. The pure romantic ideal may actually happen once in about 657,000 times, but for the rest of us, it's always at least a bit ambiguous.

Most young women of my acquaintance can't see guys other than the one they're with. Usually that means that if they're thinking about and looking at other guys, it means they're not interested in the one they're with. This isn't always true, and it might not be a good indicator in your case. It's only a general clue at best, but there are some other considerations. Perhaps you're the kind of woman who can't be satisfied with any one guy for very long. If this is true, you'll find out over a goodly stretch of time and over a long trail of boys' broken hearts. On the other hand, if you're NOT sure you DON'T want to stay with him, then don't leave him. Better not kiss any other guys, though; it'll get back to him eventually, and that'll cause the worst possible scene.

This is my most important advice, however: I most earnestly encourage you to stay faithful to the guy you're with until you leave him. I promise you that using one guy to start up a relationship just in order to get out of the one you're in is foolish for at least two good reasons. One is that if you don't give the relationship you've got your full attention, it hasn't got a chance, and you'll get into the habit of being distracted in your relationship and you'll never find a good one. Second is that the guy on the outside you get involved with looks good only as a contrast to the guy you're going with, and when you get out of the first relationship, the second guy looks entirely different… just about always. Remember that if it were the reverse — if you got involved with a married man and he divorced his wife and married you — you'd always think that what he did to his wife he'd do to you.

Act with integrity, and you'll attract people with integrity.[373]

*

As ol', dear Will used to say: the course of true love ne'er did run smooth. (I think he meant smoothly, but who's checking?)

I am more and more convinced as life goes on that it's foolish to have two serious relationships going at once. I won't say it's impossible to go beyond one-on-one, but I've never heard first — or second — hand about successful three-way relationships of any kind, at least past the very short run.[374]

*

As the man says, you pays your money and takes your choice. The perfect thing might actually happen; I've heard rumors to that effect, but if it's real, it's about a 1-650,000 chance. For the rest of us, it's always at least a bit iffy. Then, too, there is the statistical report that arranged marriages are happy in just about the same proportion as self-selected ones. That indicates to me that it's a bit of a crap shoot in any case. But here's a thing or two:

Relationships are, to a certain extent, an effort to make right what felt wrong growing up, and since everybody felt something wrong growing up, everybody carries with them the ideal of what it *should* have been like, and they carry hope for that in a serious relationship. Of course, it never works out as per the dream. In fact, your job in a relationship is to find what's up with YOU! Every time you sense something wrong in the relationship, it's a part of yourself whose expectations weren't met. Then comes the question of: are you going to insist on having those expectations fulfilled, or are you alternatively going to examine the expectations and see whether you can live comfortably *without* their being fulfilled? Mind you, there's no judgment on the point. If you can't live without certain of your needs being met, and they aren't being met, nor does it look like they ever really will be, you have to move on. No shame. You must take care of yourself in just about all circumstances, finally, because you are the only one who can.

There will always be adjustments in any relationship. Only you can determine whether the fulfillment and joy you may also have are worth the dislocation.[375]

*

It seems so strange. You don't say why on earth two people who regard each other as soul-mates would want to break up. This raises serious questions in my mind about what you and he were thinking.

What I guess I'm saying is: sure you'll find another soul-mate, no doubt, but what's to prevent you from breaking it off with him, too?

(Incidentally, you may already have noticed that having a soul-mate doesn't mean you don't have to do that hard work relationships always involve. Perhaps you were hoping for or expecting the effortless relationship, that "perfect one" that seems to lie beyond the riding off together into the sunset...?)

But to answer your question directly, how one moves on from something that may not happen again is to find some other thought to substitute for that mournful, "It may not happen again." If you hang on to that formulation, it will poison your present. Try: "Not bad, but let's see if we can't do even better." Or maybe: "God must have some wonderful plan for me. Can't wait to find out what it is."[376]

*

If a heterosexual person isn't turned off by the thought of homosexual acts, why do you suppose a homosexual person would be turned off by the thought of heterosexual acts?

This is what you're in a relationship for, to find out how to *relate*, how to *deal* with this kind of stuff. Is there a way where she can have what she wants and you can have what you want? Or not.

Compromise. Find a place to win. My only thought: the only thing that makes a relationship impossible is if one person, or the other, refuses to do the work.[377]

*

There used to be this wonderful book called *Games People Play*, by a guy named Eric Berne. And it's all about tokens, it's the way we avoid dealing in deep relationships. One of the games is: "Now I've got you, you son-of-a-bitch."

It's like I'm drawing lines in the sand and she's wandering over them, innocently enough, she doesn't know that's what they're there for: "Aha! Now I've got you."

Somebody steps over a line you've drawn in the sand and you are suddenly given the "right" to go off on them with as much venom as you've got at your command.

And then I observe the wreckage of my behavior afterward, and I go, "Jesus Christ. Can I ever pick up the pieces of this stuff?"[378]

*

You know, as I'm sitting here, typing away, I realize that, while it seems better to be the dumper, it's actually better to be the dumpee in any break-up. That's because if you give your relationships everything, I mean everything you've got, you'll walk away if the other shuts you down knowing you did absolutely everything you could. If you're willing to give that much to a relationship, you'll attract people who want that in their relationships, and who are likelier to give it all they've got.

Again and again, my message is, behave as you'd like to be behaved towards. Not so original, actually, but truer for me the older I get. Putting it into practice, now, well, I get that it's far from easy.[379]

*

Do you have a cordial, warm relationship with your man? Can you ask him directly for input? I think the idea would be not to ask him what's wrong, because that puts the situation in an either-or, right-or-wrong mode. Ask him instead, for example, what he wants out of the marriage and whether there are any accommodations possible. He is your partner until further notice, and it's a situation where you might be able to work it out if you handle the problem as something facing the partnership rather than one of you facing the other. See what I mean? It might take some time to get through the situation without having to resort to antagonism or downright fights, but if you can get to a counselor or other therapist, that would certainly help, and there are probably dozens of books in the self-help section of your local bookstore that would shed light on the situation.

Oh, yeah, and one more thought: if you just want to get laid, then, by all means, impose, impose, impose. He may actually thank you for it.[380]

*

Real life sometimes is passionate and romantic. It's true that sometimes life is bleak. Note that that's what's going on here; it's his preferences [to sexual intimacy] vs. yours. I won't pretend to know every possible way to approach the situation, but the two main topic headings are the *external*, what we call objective, and *internal*, subjective approaches.

As to the external, let's assume for the sake of discussion that you're fine, and it's all him. My take then would be that there are three main ways to go here. The first is to accept your husband as he is with all that means. (There are two subsets here, depending on your codes: you can live without physical demonstrations of affection or get them on the side. Incidentally, while I'm thinking about that, the second sub-option doesn't necessarily mean finding sexual satisfaction outside the marriage; there's a wide range of physical affection that does not step outside the normal bounds of marriage.) The second option is to get out of the marriage, and enjoy what affection you may find in the singles world, and/or get involved with someone who does behave as you'd like. (Watch out here, though, you know pitfalls await the unwary in this department.) Thirdly, and maybe the most wearying, is to get yourself and your husband into a counseling situation. Pastor, shrink, MFCC, whatever. This one's tough, because if he doesn't see any need to change, you have to provide him with reasons. Like, maybe, he won't have a marriage at all if he doesn't.

Divorce is a bitch, as anyone knows, and the woman still takes the brunt of it, though that's generally getting a bit better, but if your husband doesn't think that your preferences and desires constitute any reason for him to reconsider his attitudes, you might be better off in every way out of the marriage. I mean, you can hardly get less affection if you never get another hug in your life, can you?

Okay, that's the "change the world" approach. You know what's coming next, don't you? Yeah, sorry, it's about checking *yourself* out. Here the field is vastly more complicated, and potentially vastly more rewarding. Here the questions to ask yourself are more unsettling. Here's where you plumb the depths of your entire life. Not much to ask, is it? *Smile*

Someone once told me that if you don't know what to do, it's because you don't know who you are. As I've mentioned before, this one sticks with me. You're upset with your husband. That, I am sure, means that he's breaking some (maybe hidden) rule/s of yours. What is that rule, what are those rules? Where did you get those rules? What would happen if you abandoned those rules? (Will your entire world come crashing down around your ears?) This road is a long and difficult one. It re-engages parental issues. (What did it take to get along in your family of origin?) Did you think you deserved a reward for having done right for the last 30 years? (I'm not saying you don't, I'm just suggesting you ask yourself whether what's going on is about your entitlement.)

How have you been assuaging your sense of lack? I'll bet you've developed some habits which are not actually supportive of you.

Alcohol was my compensatory habit, numbing my feelings of not being truly noticed or regarded. Of course, it really only served to take me away from my own life, not make it better. I didn't know this at the time, finding out only in a supported abstinence. Do you have any such behaviors? Over-eating, shopping unnecessarily, fixing other people, all these serve the same purpose: distracting oneself from one's life. BTW, these may not be fixable without help; seek counsel in your community, and if you don't have one, check out the nearest appropriate anonymous, 12-Step group.

Because, it is in one's own life that, finally, all these issues are settled. Don't let me discourage you from the effort, either. The joys and rewards are boundless, a veritable cornucopia of adventure and delight, and up ahead, a better world than you ever let yourself even dream of. Hang in there, do the work, and watch your cosmos change.[381]

*

I am so sorry to hear of your separation and divorce. I am sad to say that I know of nothing that will make this time in your life easy. The worst part about it is that you have very little control over how nasty your soon-to-be-ex is going to be. You do, however, have some measure of control over your own behavior.

Some years ago there was a movement afoot to separate assertiveness from aggressiveness, which I heartily endorse to this day. "Why Do I Say Yes When I Mean No," is, I believe the name of one book that tackles this subject. [*Why Do I Say Yes When I Need To Say No? Escaping The Trap Of Temptation* by Michelle McKinney Hammond. Or, *Don't Say Yes When You Want to Say No: Making Life Right When It Feels All Wrong* by Herbert Fensterheim and Jean Baer.] In any case, the point is to decide what's best for your daughter and yourself and insist on that without becoming in the slightest nasty, demeaning or vengeful. It isn't easy, and you'll probably fail at it at times, but don't take any slip-up as a sign that it's of no use. It's of enormous use. For one thing, it'll keep your daughter from having to decide that one of you is a saint and the other a devil incarnate.

Gather all the help you can. Girl friends, family, church and therapy groups, all these will help you get through this. Just do your absolute level best to avoid blaming or name-calling during your discussions, because that will just totally diminish your stature. You want to raise a young girl with no bitterness, and you will fail if you allow yourself to become bitter.

What I am sure about heartbreak is that you will be glad one day that this is behind you, both in the sense of: "Whew, I'm glad that's over," and "I'm so happy I'm not involved in that anymore." In the meantime, take exquisite care of yourself.

Remember you're no good for anybody if you're not good to yourself.[382]

Tork About Sex

The Don And Mike Celebrity Sex Quiz, July 2001

If there is a question that is objectionable to you, Peter, you simply say, 'I decline to answer,' and we will take it as a yes.

I refuse to answer on the grounds it might incriminate me? Okay, you're incriminated.

Have you ever been involved in a three-way or enjoyed group sex?

Sure.

Have you ever had sex with a woman while she was menstruating?

Sure.

Have you ever had a homo experience?

Yes.

Have you ever made love in your parents' home?

Of course.

Have you ever enjoyed hot, interracial sex?

Yes, and cool, and in the middle, too.

Have you ever J.O'd in front of others?

Have I ever done what?

J.O.'d. Pleasured yourself.

Oh. Hmmm… J.O.'d in front of others… Yes, but only once when I was very young.

Have you ever had sex in a public place?

No.

Have you ever been filmed or photographed while having sex?

No.

Have you ever had sex in the 'no-no'?

You guys are too elliptical for me. What the hell is a 'no-no'?

You know, the back door, shall we say.

Oh... in which direction? A pitcher or a catcher?

Either.

Well, of course.

Have you ever caught?

No.

Have you J.O'd today?

No. Not yet.

Have you had sex in a car?

On a car?

In a car.

In a car, sure.

Have you ever had a one night stand, or sex with a stranger?

No. I knew all their names at all times. Do you mean, somebody's name I actually didn't know, we just went at it without finding out? Nothing like that, no. I'm too much of a gentleman for that.

You can round this off, Peter, to the nearest ten, fifty or one hundred — What approximately is your total number of sexual partners?

Well over a hundred.

Would it be under two hundred do you think?

I imagine so.

How about one-fifty?

Something like that.

*

Actually, Janis and I knew each other before we both broke, before either of us broke. I was a busboy and a beer jerk at a pub called the Golden Bear in Huntington Beach, California. I had just gone to California. And Janis was in Big Brother and the Holding Company, and they were a pretty well-known San Francisco band, but Janis hadn't broken as big as she became later. And they came through, and Janis and I just fell to talking. We had a lot in common, I mean, there was something in common.

I spoke to her about her drinking, I said, "You might get sclerosis."

She said, "*Cirrhosis!*"

I got corrected. I didn't mind being corrected. And we just became... pretty close. We lost contact. Then, a couple of years later, The Monkees were already rolling, I'm watching *2001: Space Odyssey* [released on April 2, 1968], and Janis is in the audience, too, and she, "Hey! How ya doing?" She's so raucous, you know, "Hey, how ya doing, honey?" She was fabulous. And so we hung.

What happened was, Big Brother was playing New York, and I was in New York, as I recall, and so, you know, I called her up and said, "I'm around." So she came up and hung out... And we go there, and, yeah, I... Janis, you know, retires, "I'll be there in a minute," and I walked in, we had some conversation and...

You laid the lumber. Lucky you. You're something special.

I am.

Only one time?

Twice.

Twice?

Yeah.

She came back for more.

Or I did! (Laughs) Hey, a second time is a testimonial, right?[383]

*

For a while every time I saw Janis, she was happy to see me, hugged me, gave me that great big old laugh, and the next thing I knew we were rolling in the hay together. Then one day I caught up with her at a Who concert and she wasn't friendly to me at all, and I said, "Okay, I get it, she's after one of these *other* guys!" That was that.[384]

*

There were a couple ladies living at my house, none of whom you would have heard of, probably. They'd gotten into the scene. One of them was a lady whose first encounter, I think, was with Chris Hillman, and whose second encounter was me, and whose third encounter was Peter Fonda, except that she got it on with Crosby on the side, because nobody cared in those days. So in a sense, it was groupies, but not the "pick 'em up" groupies on the street. These had actually evolved into ladies of position in the scene. Invaluable, really. Couldn't carry on without them.[385]

*

You're feeling romantic. The question really is, I think, the whole thing hinges on the *exclusivity*. I mean, he didn't want to be in this anymore. Is he saying that he's personally convinced that he can't be friends with you if you guys are sleeping together?

I've had friends that I've slept with and stayed friends, and friends that have stopped being friends because I've been sleeping with them — it works both ways. And the older you get the easier it is to find the blend.[386]

*

A couple of points come to mind. Firstly, anyone who can't stand your history doesn't deserve you, plain and simple. Secondly, however wrong it may be to lie, a full disclosure of the truth is not always a great virtue either.

More importantly, though, is what I believe I notice: that you seem to select people to whom it makes a big difference what your past is. I note that people often — make that *always* — pick people who will validate their self-image. In other words, and to go straight to the point, I expect you believe that you were *wrong* to have been as promiscuous as you were. You consequently select possible partners who validate this notion.

I am not of the school that says how you behaved was wrong. The Zen master said, "There is no right or wrong, but there are consequences." Your promiscuity was a consequence of a repressed upbringing, and it is only completely human to go too far in one direction after being held too far in the other. You behaved as you did for real, human reasons, and I say it makes perfect sense. You might not want to behave that way now, but that doesn't make you a bad girl for having behaved as you *did*.

There are millions of perfectly upright, mature and potentially loving guys who don't care about your past, as long as they have reason to believe that you will treat them and yourself with respect and honest partnership.

Hold your head up, and as far as those people who disapprove of you goes: fuck 'em if they can't take a joke. Not literally; you're being a good girl now. Heheheh.[387]

*

I don't mean to paint such a bleak picture of it. I still felt I was in the vanguard, along with a bunch of other people. I was pretty happy. I had a circle of friends, and it was a lot of fun. God knows, I went through a lot of scenes and found out what I needed to find out, which is, for instance, that orgies are nice, but they're only temporary and they're not fulfilling.[388]

*

I couldn't deal with having them every day, mind you, but… my perfect day is waking up next to someone I like a lot, having sex a couple of times… then a cup of coffee… having sex a couple more times… ummm, strolling through some interesting city like Paris, or exploring the bluffs in Malibu. A perfect day would include some good meals and good conversation. Some TV… "West Wing", that's a good show. Then sex, and sleep. That's a perfect day. And, as Micky says, "Mother of Christ, it's good to be king!"[389]

*

If you want to have sex appeal, think beautiful thoughts inside. Beautiful faces reflect beautiful souls.[390]

Tork About Self-Worth

The previous success seemed so gratuitous, it seemed so chancy, and it served a lot of people to remind me of the randomness of it, and nobody reminded me of the coherence of it, and naturalness of it.

A lot of people said, "You're just some guy off the street." And I thought, Gee I *was* just some guy off the street.

They said, "No talent." And I thought, Well I know I'm not *really* all that talented.

They said, "Any four guys…" And I thought, Yeah…

Now, I'm thinking, Gee I beat out three of four-hundred guys at the interviews and auditions; they auditioned hundreds of guys who tried out for this thing, and I got the part. On the other hand, "Well, you just got the part because of random circumstances…"

Heavy unworthiness. Oh yeah. But I'm getting over that. Therapy.[391]

*

I don't really have a lot to compare it with, since I didn't have a normal life going on at the time to which I could refer, but at the time when The Monkees hit, the fame thing was very difficult for me. I thought that kids liked our records and that they came to the shows to hear us play the music. That's why I go to shows. I couldn't believe it.

I had pathological self value. I really didn't have a sense of it at all. I didn't get why. I thought I had been picked almost at random. I didn't have any sense of myself bringing anything except that character to The Monkees. What I thought they hired me for was that character, and I think to this day that *that* had a lot to do with it. I didn't recognize how that sprung forth from who I really am. I thought I was faking them out. I thought I was handing them a lie and they were buying the lie — and so how could I value myself?

Any time you compliment somebody and they can't take the compliment, what they're saying to you is, "You don't know what you're talking about." That's the message that anybody with low self-esteem gives back when somebody compliments them. Which is where I was. All that played into this fame thing.

And it plays backwards, too. The reason that I got into the fame game was because I didn't have any sense of value. I thought, "Jeez, if I can get the millions to love me then I'll be all right."

I got the millions to love me — and it still wasn't all right. What a surprise.[392]

*

Half of the time I would think: I didn't deserve [The Monkees fame] and the other half I would think: I was God's gift to the children. I got my head turned around. It was the "arrogant doormat" syndrome, low self-esteem combined with arrogance.[393]

*

I firmly believe that a low self-esteem did not make me into an alcoholic. It's far likelier that I was born a pre-packaged dry alcoholic, and was just waiting to develop into a full-blown sopping wet alcoholic; low self-esteem was probably a function of my alcoholism, rather than the other way around.

Similarly, it wasn't reversing my low self-esteem that enabled me to get into recovery. I began my recovery after seeing, with the starkest clarity, that I was well and properly crushed by the alcoholism. It was in recovery that I began to gain any self-esteem I have now. In other words, I didn't think my way into well-being, I began to learn how to behave well and then began good thinking (*better* thinking, anyway, heheheh).[394]

*

As to my journey from self-doubt to self-esteem, I can only relate my own experience, that it was a slow process. As I think about it, I suspect that the over-all topic is too big for me to go into here. But there are some subtopic headings that just might cast some light:

Firstly, don't try to figure this out. I believe with all my heart that trying to find the reasons *why* you are as you are will avail you just about nothing. You can't think your way into right behavior, I'm sure, you must act your way into right thinking. It's possible that you're basing your observations on faulty information, but again, that won't come clear until you make a bit of progress along the path you're at the start of.

As almost always, I count the problem to be a spiritual one. (Note, please, that I'm not talking about religion, though some churches seem to be spiritual, too.) For me, spirituality means the growing awareness of the connection between ourselves and that which cares, shows care, for us without thought of material gain. (It doesn't have to be anything transcendent, either. A strong community, even a good therapy group could do the trick.) How to come by this spiritual connection is one of the great questions of the age. Some churches may be of use here. I get a lot out of reading and practicing Zen Buddhism (which is not a religion, at least as we usually mean that word).

If you're eating too much or too little, having sex with people you don't care about, drinking too much or doing any serious dope (including willful use of prescription drugs), gambling too much, shopping too much or spending too much or too little, there are 12-

Step groups eagerly awaiting you. Also, there's CoDA (Co-dependents Anonymous) and a couple of others, ACA for one (Adult Children of Alcoholics, but really for the children of any difficult family. I know you said your family was loving, but you may discover some hidden agendas lurking there.)

Being a hermit is almost certainly the worst approach to the issue. Too bad there isn't a Hermits Anonymous, but who would tell the hermits about it if they won't communicate with anyone? The problem, as I tried to indicate above, is that there is not enough connection with society, with others, with a circle of friends and people who love you.

Tell you what: try volunteering at a soup kitchen or other charity outlet. Rely on what those in charge there tell you about your work, and for God's sake, don't let your mind tell you that your low opinion of yourself trumps their observations.

There are a few other suggestions available to you, but the point here, I think, is for you to do something on behalf of your own value. Do something you believe to be valuable and you'll become valuable to yourself and the world.

The work you are embarked upon is the great work of the age, and if it seems difficult it's because it isn't easy. I suspect that only the continued effort, the daily search for the answers will bring any relief, and even then, maybe only in the long run. Don't let that discourage you, though; you didn't get into this situation overnight, and it'll take more than an overnight session to get out of it.[395]

*

I feel a very big responsibility in giving you an answer and I've turned it over and over in my mind. Many things you say in your letter bring back memories of my high school days! I felt much the same way you do.

You aren't alone in your idea that there has to be something else besides trying to be a carbon copy of everybody else around you. But as you now realize, during your teens you are bucking the system when you try for individuality. I don't mean this to sound hard on your friends — or rather the people you thought were your friends. Let me try to explain how I feel about it to you, and maybe it'll help.

The whole idea of peace and love as I see it is to let everybody do their thing, as long as it's not harmful to anyone else. There's nothing that says you have to agree with someone's opinion on dress, hair, politics, or the way the country is being run. If you prefer to listen to classical music instead of rock, then by all means do!

Everyone feels differently about certain things. That's what makes us all individuals, and life would certainly be dull if people agreed on everything. But to go back to what I said about "bucking the system," it is a lot harder to be entirely your own self when you are just developing your own ideas. When you are in high school, your social life becomes very important to you. How many parties you get invited to, how many phone calls and dates you have, the number of people you can call your friends are the things which make you feel like a worthwhile person, or a dropout from the human race.

You'll have to accept the fact that any deviation from the current fads of dress or conversation will place you in the category of being just a little different. It's not a bad thing to be — but it's not easy either! Your friends will not accept this from you readily, because they remember you as you were. Also, in doing our own thing you are giving them some doubts about themselves. You see, everyone knows deep down that there are some things they don't like about running with the crowd! But how easy it is to just sit back and accept, instead of branching out on their own!

As the years go by and people mature, most of them do find that they are entirely different than they were in high school. They look back, as I do, and say, "How could I have gone along with that!" It takes years and experience for people to find just exactly what they want and who they are. Unfortunately, too many never do!

That's why you should consider yourself lucky. You aren't really an outcast, you know. The most important person you have to please is *you*! And obviously you are trying to find the right road that brings out the self you are most comfortable with. You have to realize that you are maturing more rapidly than some of the others in your age group. It is a very important thing that is happening inside of you. You're questioning the "taken for granted" things and beginning to think for yourself. All this takes a great deal of courage and faith.

You'll find yourself asking a hundred times a day, "Do I really want this? Do I believe in this?..." and little by little you will be happier within yourself. If you keep an open mind about things, and this means not putting down the people you think have square ideas, you will find attitudes changing toward you. Remember that everybody, even those you know are wrong, do have just as much right to the ideas and way of life as you have! You can be absolutely certain that the way you feel is right — FOR YOU! What is right for someone else is their own decision.

You can argue a point of disagreement with someone by offering your views in a calm, friendly way. Don't fight about it! Don't try to force your beliefs on others, because this only antagonizes them. Everybody has to come along at his or her own pace and trying to prod or push them only makes them angry with you!

Think about what I've told you and try your very best to be open, cheerful and friendly with everyone. That includes people who have or will try to point you in one way or another. If someone puts you down, letting it roll off your back is not accepting it so much as recognizing the fact that it's their hangup, not yours! There are going to be people who will become your friends. Some of them you'll get to know, and others will find you. Your social life will pick up again, but this time you'll be doing it on your own terms! This much I know is true, because it happened to me!

The transition from being one of the crowd to being your own individual self is painful, but the way you feel about yourself is the most important thing that will ever happen to you![396]

*

Everything I hear on the subject tells me that making a gratitude list actually keeps one/me in a better frame of mind. I don't gloom out everyone around me as much.[397]

Tork About the Sixties

I arrived on the Village scene the winter of '61, and stayed there for about two and a half years. I played guitar and banjo. I came to the Village for glamour, excitement, hippiedom, the liberal lifestyle, free love. I was on the basket-passing circuit in the smaller clubs, like the Basement, the Cyclops and the Id. I later played Gerdes.

What I was working towards was to be in a group. When the Beatles hit, where were all the folkies going to go? But I also wanted to be a folk music performer.

A lot of what I did was hanging out, feeling for the first time that I was part of the scene, walking down the street and seeing people I knew, doing a little flirting. People were coming to the Village to sit down and have a cup of coffee and hope to find the free love that was supposed to be all around. The character that I was on The Monkees was developed on the stages of the Village clubs.[398]

*

I remember a Thanksgiving Day when the air was crystal clear in a way that I've never seen it before or since in LA and you could see all the way out to Catalina. It was wonderful. That crystal clarity symbolizes the whole era for me.[399]

*

Whether I believe in the "Hippie ideal" depends on your definition. I will tell you that I absolutely believe in community cooperation as opposed to top-down, autocratic rule.

And I believe that no single dogma contains the truth, at least in the literal sense.

As to my [Monkees] fortune, well, it left because I wasn't ready for it.[400]

*

I won't go nearly so far as to say that everything that came up in the 60's was valid, but as far as I'm concerned, the 60's were to what will come as Greece was to democracy. Remember that in the 60's the political officeholders had lost all touch with the needs of the nation… kind of like the Bush administration now. Back then the voice of the establishment, Life magazine, was discovered to have doctored photos falsely indicating that LSD caused chromosomal damage. That proved what we (then) kids already knew: that those at the top preached fair play and honesty, but had no more need to *honor* those concepts than what would give them the next dollar without too much trouble.

We saw perfectly clearly that we were on our own, that no one in authority cared about us. Now, like any bunch of kids left to their own devices, some, many, went off the rails. Every false step by somebody walking around under the cloak of the liberal hippy 60's was used as a pretext for dissing the entire generation. Those of us who were truly interested in liberty, fraternity and equality, however, knew we were onto something good and real. What had been called "democracy" was, and to some extent still is, a pretext for wrapping the will of the greedy and aggressive in a mantle of public acquiescence. Now, the business of wresting power away from those who make a specialty of wielding it will be a long and protracted struggle, with a lot of setbacks along the way. The outlines of the new style of governance are only dimly perceivable, and won't become clear for a long time to come. In the meantime, our job is to practice the principles of fairness and service to the best extent possible.

Hanging together in brother and sisterhood is so happy-making you want to sing right out loud.

Yeah, I feel the same about those ideas as I did then… in case you couldn't tell. Heheheh.[401]

*

You began to find what we call lame heads. At first "head" was a compliment. Anybody who smoked grass was all right with me. I saw it as a vindication of my way of life. Then I began to perceive that it was not a matter of everybody finally waking up to themselves, but rather of simply following the style of the day.[402]

*

One thing I have come to believe in recent years is that "[natural] assumptions" set us up for falls. Humans are human, and I know of no organization which makes people behave better than they did before, except maybe Alcoholics Anonymous, but that's because they stopped getting drunk and making fools of themselves. Even there, however, there are cliques, a measure of class consciousness and some continued misbehaviors (probably less so than in other places, but...!).

I will share this: during the 60's, when it was all love and peace and flower power, I thought the people had woken up and all was going to be well. It turned out that there were a couple of things wrong with that notion. One of them was that many folks jumped on a bandwagon for the fun it looked like, without taking care of some important things, like respect and careful concern. Another thing that happened is that it also looked like a threat to some other people, people with money and power, and they made it a point to mess with us. The result was that the flower power movement decayed and disintegrated. In addition, it should be said that the flower power kids weren't thinking about how to establish anything of substance. The 60's were in some measure strictly a reaction against the PTSD of the returning WWII G.I.'s, and their need for order, so it's not surprising that there was no structure with which to respond to the buffeting winds of fear and entropy.

I say this only to say that groups get together for many reasons, and it's not surprising if they don't suddenly find how to behave with total love and acceptance. If you are not permanently scarred, you might consider yourself lucky and count yourself the somewhat chastened possessor of some very valuable information.[403]

*

Yeah, that [being mobbed by fans, and sudden fame in general] was a little difficult. I didn't get it then — what it was all about and why things went the way they did. I get it now. It took me a long time to put it into some kind of order that I could deal with. I basically figure now that American kids — well, Euro-American kids — of all stripes were severely repressed. I mean, all cultures repress their people to some extent, and I think ours does just as good a job as any. Particularly in the '60s, they were so severely repressed because those were the children of people who grew up in the '40s; it was World War II, post-war peace and prosperity. These are the people who raised these kids, and they expected: "We did right in the world, so we can tell you what to do." And nobody is paying any attention to the kids. The post-war head mindset was losing its steam, but nobody noticed. That's why they went into Vietnam; they thought they were fighting another war to end all was. But it really was just some people saying, "Well, it's our turn to fight. We wanna fight a war.

We wanna lead a war." It was just the next half-generation screwing up. So along come these freedom-looking kids (The Monkees) on this television thing, whose idea was to project freedom and fascination and danger and adventure and fun and music. It was enough to make you just lose your little heart.

So these kids who screamed at us — basically it was out of their repression toward their dream of freedom, which we stood for. They didn't know it at the time. We didn't know this at the time. Nobody knew this. It was way beyond any information. But this is what happened, I think.

All I knew was that they were screaming and wouldn't shut up and I was playing music, and I thought I was a hot musician![404]

*

Oh, I thought the New Dawn had come. The Dawning of the Age of Aquarius. So did everybody else. We thought everything was just going to be roses from here on out. But you have to do that. Those of us who were young and innocent and open and thrilled to be part of the age were not able — couldn't have mustered the vision — to see that it was a passing thing and that it would eventually turn around.[405]

*

When they shot them down at Kent State, that was the end of the flower-power era. That was it. You throw your flowers and rocks at us, man, and we'll just pull the guns on you. Essentially, the revolution, which was sort of tolerated as long as it wasn't a significant material threat, was not tolerated anymore. And everybody went "Oops" and scurried for cover and licked their wounds. They became isolated — which was the point of it all.

"Togetherness isn't going to get it," was the moral they tried to lay on us, because the less togetherness there is, the more room there is for exploitation.

Kent State was an attempt. Let's try this and see what happens. And what happened was the shooting and vast inflation and a swing to the right — the moral majority. The whole thing was inherent in the situation. A certain amount of loosening up, a certain amount of extra leisure, and people are going to try to improve their lot instead of just barely hanging on. If you had a little extra you're going to try to make everything better. And if you see that your own happiness, or the lack of it, is tied in with the sadness of your neighbor, you're going to start feeling communal. And that's going to expand until the crunch comes. As long as people are educated to believe that isolated self-interest is the only way to go, when the crunch comes they'll withdraw from each other. And only now, in the faintest glimmerings, do I see any sense that people are realizing that togetherness and flower power alone won't get it. It's got to be togetherness, flower power, *plus* a willingness to do something pretty stern from time to time. If you're not willing to behave sternly, people who won't stop short of stern behavior are going to keep on going. It's taken a while for that message to sink in.[406]

*

I didn't have any sense of that at the time [that I was part of a young elite hanging out with some pretty heavy hitters]. I didn't know they were members of the elite until years later when they all had successful careers. I didn't know Richard Havens was doing really well. I didn't know José Feliciano was making it. I didn't know any of those guys were going to be good until they got good, so it wasn't like I was hanging out with heavy hitters, as far as I knew at the time.[407]

*

Hendrix was a sweetie. He was an absolute champ. Humanly, he was a total champ. You could say anything to him about his guitar work or about yours, ask him any question, and he would stop and he'd answer you seriously. He never threw me off, he never shortchanged me with his time. Anything I had to say to him, anything I wanted to talk to him about, he was there. He was an absolute champ. They don't come any better.

No, [I was not surprised when Jimi eventually quit the tour] — I knew it couldn't happen, it wasn't working for him. I was sad to see him go because he was such an inspiration musically, one of the best musicians I've ever heard in my life, and I truly believe that they have not caught up to Jimi as a guitar player yet today.[408]

*

It was a long time between when I last saw Buddy [Miles] and when he died. I hadn't heard from him, nor, as far as I know, he about me, for years. When we did spend time together, back in the late 60's, we were pretty close for a little while, but didn't keep much track of each other after I left Hollywood.

I first saw him playing drums for the great Electric Flag, the best of the horn rock bands, as far as I'm concerned. They were playing at the Monterey Pop Festival, and Buddy was huge at the time. I don't think he ever got slim, but he was certainly much slimmer when I hung with him later.

He was a splendid drummer, and I was able to get him into the studio to do a few cuts with me. Nothing much ever came of it, but if you find "Seeger's Theme" in one of those Monkee outtake collections, that's him playing drums. He was also a very good singer, and even took up the guitar a bit, bending notes in the most soulful way.

I guess the fact that he played drums with Jimi Hendrix was the best testament to his skills.

If there's an afterlife of any kind, he's still at it.[409]

*

George [Harrison] invited me to play banjo on Wonderwall. He was working on the soundtrack for Wonderwall, and he invited me to come and play, and I did. You can't hear it on the album, you can't hear it on the album, but apparently — and I never have seen the movie — it's in the film.

I think it was Paul's banjo. Paul had a five-string banjo, which he had strung backwards of course, being left-handed. But it was all right with him if I restrung it. So… and British five-string banjos are different from American. The fifth string, instead of having a tuning peg right in the middle of the neck, it hits a tunnel and the string goes through a tunnel to a fifth string peg at the regular peg head. Very interesting, very weird. But it was okay. Got some music in, that's all that mattered.[410]

*

George Harrison invited me to his house. He played the sitar and said: "I'm working on a soundtrack album, I'd love to have you play a little banjo."

I played for 45 minutes, George said, "Thanks very much," and we went our separate ways.

And I did not get paid. George said: "We'll figure that out later." He knew that the honor itself was payment enough![411]

*

I was very lucky to have been able to see the bands you mentioned, and many more, in my days in that world. You ask me who shoulda been huge, and I have to say that Traffic never got its due, as far as I'm concerned. When Dewey Martin died just recently, his obit mentioned that he was the drummer for a relatively low-visibility group, but I always thought Buffalo Springfield was one of the greats. So did Ahmet Ertigun, who signed them to Atlantic Records, and so did George Harrison, to my direct knowledge. I thoroughly enjoyed The Electric Flag, starring such luminaries as Michael Bloomfield on guitar, Buddy Miles on drums, Harvey Brooks on bass and Nick Gravenitis on vocals. I saw them at the Monterey Pop Festival, and thought they were great! It seems that drugs took them out. Let that be a warning to you youngsters: stay away from drugs! Fat lot of good that will do.

The list of overlooked talent, then as now, is too long to begin to cover. I could only touch on the subject, but thanks for asking; you sent me to a good place.[412]

Tork About Sobriety

I am in the wonderful position of enhancing my own recovery by sharing the process with whoever will listen, so it is a great favor to me for you to ask.[413]

*

If you took a roomful of cancer victims, diabetics and alcoholics and told them that they could avert the effects of their diseases by going to a room and just listening, and sometimes talking, for an hour, four to six times a week, it's only the alcoholics that would resist the idea.[414]

*

It's not my job to take care of anybody else's sobriety — thank god — my own has been more than a handful for me, thanks very much.[415]

*

An alcoholic asked his sponsor how many meetings he went to.

"Oh, about four or six a week," said the sponsor.

"You still need that many?"

"Oh, no, I probably need only about one a week. I just don't know which one."[416]

*

I was very fortunate because I found myself to be an alcoholic and there is a community that is out to help and who will love you just because you're an alcoholic who wants to get better. That was the beginning of my retrieval as a human being. Otherwise I'd be a bubbling pile of protoplasm in the gutter someplace.[417]

*

One of the things in the "Celebrate Recovery" thing is: "I can't help behaving badly sometimes," and I think, [laughs] that's me! And I have to let go of my own will in this matter and turn to a community. Doesn't say that in the steps. The eight steps of recovery, or the twelve steps of celebrate, or the twelve steps of the anonymous systems, it doesn't say: Turn it over to your *community*. But everybody I know who has come through recovery has, at one time or another, said, "Thank god for your people. If it hadn't been for my group, I couldn't have done this."[418]

*

I hasten to add that particularly in the first year — and very much similarly to the second and third years — do nothing but stay sober. All your energies, everything, goes on the shelf.

And I did that, and I'm very grateful. I was very lucky in terms of my financial situation: I didn't need to work very much, and I was able to go a lot of meetings, and I did too — even before I got clean and dry, when I was just alcohol-free but still doing those other chemical substances — I went to a lot of meetings. I must have gone to a thousand in my first year, which is not hard to do in New York City. There were days when I would wake up and go to the nooner, and then walk uptown to the 4 o' clock meeting, and come back down for a back-to-back beginner, and regular meetings in the evening, and then go to the midnight meeting, and go home. That was my day. Many days when I would do that kind of thing. And I was just as happy as a clam, I tell you.

I love this stuff, this recovery thing, that's the fellowship and the program and talking about the real things. You know I just didn't believe that there was any place on earth where I could openly talk about the things that are taken for granted in these rooms. And I'm extremely grateful for the entire recovery fellowship process.[419]

*

Yeah, I was a serious substance abuser, I abused some serious substances — and they abused me in return, it was only fair. But I'd like to report now, for the sake of all those who care, that I haven't abused a single substance in a long time. I'm actually, I'm very happy about it, although I have to say that it has nothing to do with willpower or, you know, strength of character or any of that kind of thing, which a lot of people talk about. It was just surrender, it was just giving up.[420]

*

Somewhere along the line, it finally sunk in. Not only that I couldn't drink safely, which I knew, but that there was no pretense — no way to pretend to you or me that there was a chance of a pretense — of drinking *safely*. And somehow, that got through to me and I was able to turn and make some requests and go find the help that I needed.

So I got a community. And with a community, who had been through what I needed to go through, I was able to give up my will.

So it was no longer a matter of, "Man, what willpower you've got! You haven't had a drink in 28 years; how do you do it, man? If I had your willpower…"

Nuh-uh-uh-uh-uh. It's not *having* the willpower. It's *giving up* the willpower. It's surrendering, hopefully, to a dedicated community.

That enabled me to begin the slow process of *dealing* with all the stuff that I drank about in the first place. I knew I was a runner-away, I'd run away all the time. And that made me a cheat. And since I knew I was a cheat, I cheated. Vicious cycle. I cheat you… and then I run. I know I'm a cheat, so it doesn't matter whether I cheat, because that doesn't change anything, so I cheat and I run, and I cheat and I run.

Everything. Relationships. I was pretty good with cash register honesty, I learned that at my father's knee. But almost every emotional honesty available to me was not available to me. And I'll tell you the truth, folks, 28 years later, that emotional recovery, emotional honesty and depth is, right now, my *biggest* challenge. I ain't got it yet. It is better than it ever was, and I'm beginning to — I feel like I'm rounding a corner. Of course, I've been feeling that way for 28 years. But it feels like I'm getting better. And I know I am. The quality of my friendships is richer and deeper and stronger. My friends are more important in my life, and I'm more important in my friends' lives.

And I am able to hear when somebody says, "Is that exactly what you had in mind right there? Is that a perfectly *honest*…"

And I go, "Well, maybe not, I think I can probably do better than that." And I work on it.

In other words, because I have what I can rely upon, I am able to get better. And getting better enables me to stay sober. Staying sober enables me to get better. And that cycle — which was a vicious cycle before — is now a benign cycle. And it's taking me to some really wonderful places.[421]

*

It's been 26 years since I had anything willingly, and when I tell people this, sometimes they go, "Gosh man, you must have a hell of a lot of willpower."

And I tell them, "No, it's not about willpower. In fact, it's exactly the opposite."

As long as I was relying on willpower, I was doomed. I was absolutely doomed. It wasn't until I was able to surrender my willpower and ask for help that I was able to quit that which I was not wanting to partake in for three to five years. I'd been trying to quit drinking for three to five years and I couldn't do it until I really hit bottom and became painfully and excruciatingly aware that I had no further control, and then I was able to surrender and get the help I needed. And it's been a function of the help and not the willpower. So this is word to the wise if anybody is interested in what's going on with their lives and why they keep on behaving in ways they don't understand. It's not up to me to change my own behavior, it's up to accepting guidance, really, from… I don't want to go into names here — there are people who will use words to tell you where the guidance is coming from, and I don't want to do that particularly — but I had to surrender to something or someone that knew better than I did how to do it for me. And with that in hand I've been able to stay sober all this time. And it's been, oh god, it's been a blessing, I'm telling you![422]

*

What I can tell you is that willpower kept me drunk. The more willpower I laid on myself, the less happiness I got, the less sober I got. My sobriety, my recovery, depended upon *surrender*. And I see this "Celebrate Recovery" thing going around, probably attached the church here, and that's a very Christ-based operation, and the operation that I got sober in was not quite so specific. But it really was critical for me to find some kind of dependability.[423]

*

I am sure that alcoholism is a disease of isolation, and since mostly only AA's understand an alcoholic, staying away from meetings tends to promote isolation, which in turn increases the risk of a relapse. It isn't always and absolutely true, of course, but do you really want to take that one in 500 chance that you'll lead a fully conscious sober life *without* meetings? Make meetings. If you pay attention, I believe you'll find that they seem to add time to your day.[424]

*

It is true that I have managed, one day at a time, to refrain from acting out on my addiction to alcohol for some number of years now, but I must tell you that all I know about it is what I've learned from others who are on the same journey. So what I have to suggest is only my understanding of whatever consensus I believe there is.

Firstly, I am not a doctor, nor are most of my fellow recovering alkies and addicts. It is pretty well agreed in my circles, moreover, that in the recovery model, there is no room for medical advice. Generally, the rule is, take what your doctor tells you to take, in the amount s/he tells you to, and don't take what s/he doesn't tell you to take, nor what is prescribed in unprescribed amounts. I have taken narcotic pain relievers from time to time, after surgeries, and my experience was that, when I kept to the dose prescribed, I didn't get a high, or a rush of any kind, or an urge for more, nor, in fact, *any* mood change at all. I have been exceedingly careful to switch to over-the-counter pain meds as soon as I was able, neither denying myself what relief from pain was available, nor looking for a drug experience. This tells me that, properly taken, pain meds, even some powerful ones, will *not* kick you back into addictive behaviors.

You may, however, not have the option to switch to milder forms of relief. I urge you to consider whether your fear of being on the prescribed pain meds is based on anything more than a wish to be drug-free. I thought I heard you say just that you didn't want to be on them in ten years. I wouldn't either, but you may have no choice, and I hope you'll bear your cross with reasonable good cheer. Just keep consulting with your pain control practitioner, and keep up with developments in the field.

Oh, by the way, one thing, not meant as a substitute for meds, but perhaps as an adjunct: I've had some good luck around pain with acupuncture. Check that out.[425]

*

If you were working with me on your recovery (which I hope you have a real, live, close-up person for), I would make sure that you did step work. You're not going to get to the forgiveness part of the program until you do the work around joining the group, finding a higher power and doing an inventory. Just about no one has the power to do the real healing work alone. It absolutely requires assistance of your community. Okay, maybe not absolutely, but are you going to take the one in 500,000 chance that you're the spiritual genius who's exempt? I didn't think so. Good.

You say it's been 30 years, but if you're having a hard time letting go, then it doesn't matter how long it's been. I believe you're in some trouble, and I urge you to restart the steps of the anonymous program(s).

The only requirement incumbent upon you in the meantime is that you don't act out. Don't pick up a drink or a drug, don't go raging at anyone if you can possibly, possibly prevent it. Stick with the program, and you'll get to the later stuff later.

Stay with it, live long and prosper![426]

*

When I got sober, I began to face the life I had been avoiding all those years. After all, I mean, I didn't drink for no reason. I drank for a reason.

Everybody grows up with two statements in their heads. One is true, and the other's a lie.

The true one is: you can't do this without help.

The lie is: There's *no* help.

If you wake up with that one — *there is no help* — then what are you gonna do *but* drink? "You'd drink too if you had my problems." Which is the usual cry.

And it turns out that we *can* do this, with help. And that's the glory of recovery. So with the fellowship and the program, slowly, the process begins.[427]

*

One on one help with a therapist is usually not good enough, it has to be at least in a group with a co-therapist, a man and a woman, or ACA (Adult Children of Alcohol), which is really Adult Children of dysfunctional families, some children of non-alcoholic dysfunctional families belong there. You're never gonna learn how to fix this by yourself, honest to god, you have to get community help. ACA. Go to a lot of meetings until you find a meeting that you like.[428]

*

I will recommend Overeaters Anonymous. I've never been there myself, not having a food problem (so far as I can now see), and I've heard mixed results from some people, but I've also seen and heard of huge successes. One woman told me she'd kept off 100 pounds for seven years! (Incidentally, it's not just for overeaters, it's for anyone whose relationship to food is other than for satisfying hunger.) It would be important to get to a lot of meetings, and if you don't enjoy any one meeting after going a half a dozen times, go to lots of others. Go to a ton of meetings before you beGIN to try to imagine thinking about making the hint of the very start of a decision.[429]

*

It is [a day-to-day thing], or should I say that it serves me better to think of it that way. I don't know what it is, and what isn't, but if I start thinking, "Well, I don't have to worry about this..." I've heard too many stories about too many people who didn't worry about it because they were fine, and the next thing you know they were drinking. Or maybe even worse, you know, or dry drunks, where they're snarling and nasty to people and *not* drinking, you know? People like that... "Jesus, have a drink for Christ sakes!"[430]

*

You have nothing to fear, here. You have a chance to behave well today, and on into the foreseeable future. Don't drink and drive anymore, for starters, and you can probably assume a decent life for yourself in relatively short order.

One more thing; if you can't stay dry, better get your ass to some AA meetings. You have ample reason to know that you can't drink safely.[431]

*

Go [to AA meetings], by all means, go. Here's why: Anybody there, is there for the same reason, so they're certainly not going to judge you. Perhaps your substance abuse has been made public by your own behavior, and the people there are only going to applaud you for doing something about it. BTW, if it's primarily alcohol, or alcohol and pot, go to AA. If there are other, hard drugs involved, go to NA (Narcotics Anonymous). They do understand, after all; they're all going through it, too.

A lot of the behavior you mention (fighting with parents and friends) is very likely the outgrowth of your chemical abuse, and if not, it is a byproduct of whatever is making you use and abuse substances in the first place. Also, the chances of some busybody — none of whose business it is — seeing you go into those meetings is very small, actually.

So let me repeat: Go, girl, go.[432]

*

I am an alcoholic, and I don't believe I'm any less of an alcoholic than I was when I put down the chemistry 27+ years ago. In fact, alcoholism is a progressive disease; if you resume drinking, you don't pick up where you left off, you pick up where you would have been if you'd been drinking continuously all the while. The evidence for this is conclusive, in my judgment.[433]

*

Here's one more little thing, what most people don't realize is that for alcoholics of my type, if you are abstinent — if you're clean and dry for a number of years — and you take up drinking again, you don't take up drinking where you left off. Within a very short time you are where you would have been if you'd been drinking continuously in between. So if you're on a long down slope, and you get off it, and five or ten years later you get back on it, you are much worse and much further down the slope than you were when you left off. So if I took up drinking right now, I would be — I've heard stories of people who lost their houses, their wives, their homes, their job, their car, their career, their money, everything gone within two or three days of picking up. So I hope I never do, because if I do I'm bloody doomed I'm telling you.[434]

*

This is part of my growth. I have to keep growing in order to stay sober. And that's the final lesson, the final point of all this stuff: *I got sober in order to lead my life, and I lead my life in order to stay sober.* It's a wonderful combination because the opposite — the vicious circle that was dragging me down — was also true: *I got drunk in order to avoid facing my life, and I avoided facing my life in order to drink.*[435]

Tork About Spirituality

Cosmic intelligence, higher power, connectedness, the pattern, the source – these are ways of alluding to the process that expresses itself, in my experience, as intelligence and order. So we discuss a source, an unknowable source, which we call one, the unified one, from which all things spring.[436]

*

I'm a Buddhist, and a Christian, and a Hindu, and a Jew, and… like that. You don't go to heaven because you're a Buddhist… You're *in* heaven because you're a Buddhist.[437]

*

All the Eastern religions have a great deal in common. They all believe that your reward and punishment is a direct result of your own behavior. For instance, if you're smiling at somebody and making them happy you're in Heaven.[438]

*

Then a miracle happened. I found, "The Difference." I can't name "The Difference" for a dozen reasons, one of which is that no name sounds the same to everybody. If I said, "God," a lot of people — a previous self of mine included — would say, "Oh, spare me your sanctimonious bull." If I say, "the cosmic patterning," then it would be "Oh, spare me your hippie-dippy bull."

Okay. Call it "The Difference" and be done with it.

What difference did it make?

I was crazy. I was behaving crazily. It wasn't like I was a moral leper. I was just addicted and feeding my habit. Then one day I looked at the chemicals in my hand — in that case a bottle of beer — and I saw that I was not in charge. When I finally realized that, that's when I began to recover. Since then I have been able to avoid the use and abuse of all chemicals, primarily and including alcohol.[439]

*

Was I shocked when I heard Janis [Joplin] died of an overdose? No, I wasn't. Janis toyed with the extremes of life from the start, according to reports and what I knew of her, and I suspected she was using heroin. From there, it's just a matter of probably, and when, before an overdose hits. Of course, I was saddened, and I mourned. She was wonderful to know and to hang out with, and of course it was wonderful to enjoy her fabulous talent.

Meanwhile, there are answers to this problem. They're simple but not easy. The problem may be seen to be that there is no one trustworthy enough to follow. If you grow up like that, it will be very difficult to find reliable guides in this life. There is a True Guide, however. Many follow the God of their understanding. Others are so turned off by religion and all its adherents that nothing under the name of "God" will serve. That's okay; the True Guide does not have to have the title "God" to be useful. It does require an understanding of — and a willingness to — pursue whatever in life might usefully lead us to an acceptance greater than the temporary one provided by acclaim or possessions.

The understanding of this greater acceptance will come slowly, but it comes to those who are willing to keep open their eyes and minds.[440]

*

Now [Micky and I] share our religious and philosophical viewpoints, which are very similar. For instance, we both believe that God is not a man sitting on a throne somewhere. We both think that this viewpoint is simple, childish and inaccurate. Anyone who worships this sort of God is worshipping an idol, not God. We both believe that peace on Earth can only begin with "me", which is pretty much the basis of everything.[441]

*

I believe that anybody who takes an opinion somebody else has laid on them and says that it's right, anybody who believes in something without checking it out thoroughly for themselves, has a serious flaw in personality. There's no need to take anything on faith because anyone who does is depriving themselves. You can find God by the scientific method, all you have to do is do it.[442]

*

When I was a kid it started off with these questions of God, boring on me. I was always wondering, "Well, is there a God? Isn't there a God?" and my parents weren't any help. They didn't have much of a religion. It didn't bother them whether they had one or not. They didn't seem to feel there was any pressing need to answer these questions. Then I read a book called, *My Dear God*, or something like that, which for the first time proposed to me the possibility that living God is experienceable, that is, it's possible to know, to make contact with God, to see the connections. The book said that throughout history prophets have come along who have seen the connection, and who have described it in great detail, but because it's so vast and complex, ultimately the shorter-sighted disciples of theirs would not be able to keep all the pieces together and it would disintegrate. The unity of the understanding would disintegrate, and so you would begin to have sects: "So and so said…" and the other people would say, "No, he said *this*…", and in the case of Western religions, going to war over that.

Now when I read this in the book, that cleared a big blinking path out of my way. And then nothing happened until my acid trip, the big acid trip at Susan Haffie's when I went storming out the door and rolling, doing cartwheels in the pumpkin patch, or whatever it was. And I then had what might well have been hallucination, at least I had this picture. It came to me that the word "God" could apply to the sum total of benevolent intelligences, and I had a few in mind, including Theodore Sturgeon, whom I met later on, cause I read a lot of his science-fiction books, I thought he was real good. And I'd read *Stranger in a Strange Land*, which I thought was enormous, and the only book Heinlein ever wrote. I don't understand how he did it, but he tapped into something at one point and wrote this book, and it's a tremendous book, just really says what I needed to hear at the time. And then my acid trip, it came together. And after that I had a few more flashes later on where it all came together that God is not the sum total of benevolent intelligences, but that intelligence in and of itself has its own purposes and drives, and that God is intelligent, that everything has a direction to it. All events and the way things happen have a purpose and a plan, and that from time immemorial, matter has sought to become more particularly intelligent. That is that human beings are only an expression of matter's own tendencies, and this is staggering to a scientist, that matter has a tendency to want to become human.

Well, I think that that's what happens, and that's that.[443]

*

Someone recently said that people who want to talk to you about their religion rarely want to hear about yours. I am only too aware that my expressing my spiritual/religious views leaves me open to the charge of proselytizing, which I don't want to do. Everyone has to come to their own views, as far as I'm concerned, whether or not certain conventional religions provide a suitable framework.

Having said all that, though, and since you asked, I will try to give you a quick sketch. Firstly, eastern "religions" (I use quote marks to say maybe they aren't religions*) have indeed been a huge source for me. My mom gave me a book on Zen when I was in my teens, and while I didn't get much from it then, I have found in the years since that Zen Buddhism has an attitude that appeals to me a great deal, as far as I understand it. I'm something of a minimalist, I think, at least in these matters, and Zen has been about as minimal as it's possible to be and still say anything at all. Incidentally, I can also recommend anything by Krishnamurti, who might be seen as uncompromising to the limit, but he's great anyway.

I grew up in an agnostic/atheistic/non-theistic household. I wondered for years what everybody was on about when they said "God." I certainly wasn't interested in whatever religion the good boys and girls in school were into, usually Catholic, sometimes Protestant. My father didn't believe in the God he was presented with, and I don't believe in that God either. Howsoever, I do believe that awareness of a connectedness of some sort is critical to human well-being.

One Zen teacher said "Life is the teacher." That made all kinds of sense to me, because whatever we're talking about here, it has to be real. Unverifiable assertions are useless to me, so if it's real, it will show in real life, some way, somehow, some time.

Anyway, all of that is partly to say that I had no particular religion to break away from at home, except the "religion" of rationalism. I did have a set-to or two with my father about my developing sense of connection, which included phenomena he couldn't allow himself to believe were even possible. That part was tough, and we never did completely reconcile over the point, though we got along okay through the rest of his life.

As to my routine today, well, I don't believe I actually have one. My sobriety is the critical issue for me now, so I daily take a moment to consider that, and I reaffirm whatever it takes to keep me mindful. There's a strong spiritual component to recovery from addiction/alcoholism, so maybe that counts as a spiritual routine, though it seems a bit far-fetched to call it that. Mostly it's just what keeps me from acting out so badly that I begin a deteriorating slide to hell.

That's enough, by Gar!

*Some of the schools of thought I follow don't engage with the concept of God at all. Maybe better to think of them as psychologies or philosophies.[444]

*

All my life I have been interested in eastern philosophy and wisdom. I have read the writings of Tao for many years and *The Sayings of Buddha* (a small, inexpensive book you can find in almost any book store) always rests on the night-table beside my bed. I find that ancient wisdom, meditation and contemplation puts my mind in order and brings me great serenity.[445]

*

I was able to change my course as early as I did, relative to some of the stories I've heard, because of my dabblings in Eastern philosophy. Because of that spiritual experience I had beforehand on acid (which has since been validated and expanded) and because of a few experiences in community, I've been allowed to recognize that what I really did want to find on a day-by-day basis was *spiritual surrender*. Now, I am not in charge, not in the sense that somebody else is in charge, but in the sense that what is in charge is larger than I can know by myself, but I have to trust it.[446]

*

If you read [Krishnamurti] now, he'll say again and again, "Don't follow me. Don't do things because I do them. Check out what I'm saying. If it makes sense, follow the truth as you understand it. Don't listen to me. Don't listen to anybody."

And that has been a very strong beacon for me ever since. I never did fall into the sway of any guru. I was deeply distrustful of them at all times.

One big Yogi guru said to me, "We must appeal to the one who knows," and he pointed up.

And I'm going, "Is that where it all is, up there?"

I mean, some people think that God is a honky on a throne directly overhead. "Well you can't see him because the ceiling is there, but he's there, with a beard." The honky with the beard.[447]

*

Jack Nicholson (who told me not to name-drop) said that one of those spiritual teacher guys he felt made the most sense was Krishnamurti. I immediately went out and got his *Think on These Things*, and read it through. I agree with Jack that he makes a great deal of sense. Basically, what Krishnamurti says is don't take anybody's word for anything, but check it out for yourself. The speech that I said — which really wasn't how to get out of the box, but rather to see that the "box" is an internal reality — was a paraphrase of the speech the Indian guru gives in the steam room, and I'm grateful to Jack and Bob Rafelson (who co-wrote, co-produced, and directed "Head") that they didn't make a lot of fun of me. For instance, I could have repeated the guru's speech word for word, but they wrote me saying it in my own language. I actually still hold with what the speech says, which is basically that direct action does not involve choosing, but is a result of being alert to the moment.[448]

*

I think the most overrated virtue, generally speaking in the population, the most overrated virtue is piety. Displays of piety. People going, "Look how pious I am." I think that that is not only overrated but *dangerous*, really.[449]

*

My nourishment? I pray.

Yeah, I'm religious. I try and get in touch and stay contacted with the larger things, sure.[450]

*

I taught English and social studies. And sure, the kids probably saw me as a Monkee, but they got over that in a hurry. Once I lost my temper at the kids, they'd see I was just like all the others — and I probably lost my temper too many times, since I was in an angry state back then. I have a life now, that's the difference. I have a spiritual core. I'm not Shirley MacLaine but I believe in greater or lesser worlds and consciousness. Most people think of themselves as cut off from each other; others know there's a connectedness that can be tapped into.[451]

*

Everything you do is an accumulation of everything you have done in your life. If each action could be fully understood, it would explain everything about you. That is the ideal. In everything is its opposite. If you curse with great violence, there's a tiny spot in which your gentleness appears, and if you say, "I love you," with great tenderness and passion, there is also an indication of hostility and anger.

I think a great deal about the religions of the Far East, although when I talk about them, I always feel as if I am swimming with my head just above the surface of the water, and I'm about to go under. I'm thinking all these things out and changing my ideas as I go along. I've grown a great deal in the past twelve months. What I was like at the beginning of this and what I'm like now are light-years apart. And what I'll be like when another year has passed will be even more startling. But it's not all due to the pressure of being one of The Monkees. Those pressures may have influenced the way I have changed, but I would have changed in similar ways anyhow. In the early days of The Monkees they called me a poet. "Peter Tork reads or recites his own poetry at the drop of a hat," they said, but that's not true. I don't consider myself a poetic person at all; I'm more of a "prosetic" person.[452]

*

I LOVE reading anything I can lay my hands on, but I'm particularly into far eastern philosophy. For instance, did you know that according to an ancient Upanishad... on the tree of life within us sits two birds. One eats, pecks, scratches and gets on with living in general. The other watches, always silent, always awake, always fully aware — unless you let him fall asleep. If he falls asleep, the other bird goes on pecking and scratching away without any *meaning* to his life. If *you* keep the second bird awake, he guides the first bird to higher and higher levels, so that one day they both become one being — full of bliss, consciousness and wisdom.[453]

*

And what I found was a bunch of people who had been there before me and who, gathered together, were able to keep each other sober, and in whose care I could stay sober. So it turns out that — for starters, and substantially to this day — my higher power is my community. And I get this from every religious tradition I look at: that the community is a critical aspect of recovery, whether you're recovering or just trying to get better. So for those of you who have a very specific higher power, namely the Judeo-Christian God of Abraham Isaac and — who's the other guy? [Jacob] — the biblical God, and more specifically Jesus Christ, I don't believe you get there without going through people. I don't believe it. Again, this is just me.[454]

*

I hope to see uncloudedly, that's all. And it's a skill. It's not something that suddenly you're able to do it, you know, one day your eyes are opened and the heavens sing and it's like that forever more, it's not like that. It's a skill. It comes and goes and the more skillful you are the more often it comes and the longer it stays and the more intensely you feel it, and the less skillful you are, the reverse. There's nothing to it, you just keep on doing it to the best of your ability. Actually, lovely thing, we're all on the same path, not everybody knows it. There's no, "He's not on the path." None of that.

The whole thing about spirituality is that we're in this together. Which, incidentally is one of the things about the blues, too. The blues is about, "We're all in this together" and I'm absolutely certain that "Leave all these other stupid people behind" is not spiritual, as we are using the word these days. So if you're not including everybody then you're only being partial with yourself.[455]

Tork About Trust

Don't buy lies. Don't believe everything you're told… especially when growing up. Investigate for yourself and find out the truth on your own terms.[456]

*

The only advice I want to give is to stop guessing why and whether any man would want to date you. More importantly, though, is your distrust of men. Speaking as one, I will confess that sometimes I wonder why any woman would trust any man, but it's obvious that there are trustworthy men, so I have to figure that not all men are untrustworthy.

I do my best to be trustworthy myself, but the best I can say for myself is that eventually I own up to my failings (as well as I can), and do what's possible to set things right when I've messed up.[457]

*

I imagine — this is not much more than a guess — that you've had a hard time, dating all the way back to your childhood, with this trust issue. You come from a family where betrayal was only too common a feature. Neglect and maybe even abuse occurred regularly. I'm still guessing here, but I believe that mistrust of men (or women, or people in general, for that matter) stems from childhood lessons learned badly but too well. Reordering your trust muscles can't happen overnight, or even overmonth at best, but until you can imagine that a trustworthy man is a *possibility*, you will only reaffirm your pre-assessment by picking untrustworthy men every time you select one. It's inevitable, I'm sure.[458]

*

I lie under two circumstances. One is in the greater good, 'cos there's sometimes when the honesty is not a good thing to do. And sometimes out of just screaming gibbering terror.[459]

*

However wrong it may be to lie, a full disclosure of the truth is not always a great virtue either. If a bully looking for your friend comes to your door, it's really good to lie to him, and send him off in the wrong direction.[460]

Tork About Wisdom

I enjoy passing on wisdom — it's a big part of my life. Everybody has different character traits and it's how you use them that counts. I used to be a busybody but now I help people by listening to them and helping them work things out and it's a virtue.[461]

*

A friend of mine just heard me talking to somebody, and apparently I just started to talk about this person's situation, and she thought that I went into it with a great deal of breadth and depth.

"Wow, Peter would be good at this kind of thing; let me see if we can't do something with that."

So she suggested it, and bless her, it's actually worked out. I do the whole thing: the advice to the lovelorn, and my husband doesn't look at me, and was that a Gretsch bass you were playing. There's The Monkee questions, and what was it like to do this, or how did you feel to do that, as well as the general advice to the lovelorn and people in pickles of one sort or another.[462]

*

The most satisfaction in life every day comes from being useful. I've been working really hard, gaining a lot of understanding and when somebody else can use it, I'm a happy camper. Besides the music of course, that's all besides the music, which is where it all comes from to begin with. But if you're talking about the daily person interpersonal stuff? Being of use.[463]

*

Everything I learned, I had to learn twice.[464]

Tork About Zen

My mom gave me a Zen book in my teens. I don't believe it made a real big dent, but it did open me up to the idea of Zen as it became a greater part of my life later on. I believe that the idea of meditation is to get one closer to seeing things as they are and not as our sometimes chattering mind tells us they are, which I believe is one of the most valuable lessons there is.

As to yoga itself: most mornings I do a short series of poses to stretch out and to focus a bit. As to formal meditation, while I do that, too, sometimes, it's not as regular.[465]

*

Zen Buddhism believes in the theory of sudden enlightenment or sudden awakening. This idea is Japanese. I believe that Truth can just come to you in a sudden flash and you'll know where it's all at, if you prepare yourself to receive it.[466]

*

I'm now learning to speak Japanese from the Berlitz Japanese teacher. In the Berlitz school you're only supposed to speak the language you're learning, but sometimes we talk in English too. Some of the words I've learned are "empitzu" which means "pencil," "Ohaio" which means "Hello" or "Hi", and "Nihongo" which means the Japanese language itself.

When I go to Japan I'd like to go to Kyoto most of all. Kyoto is the former capital of Japan and it's the center of the Zen Buddhists. Zen Buddhist temples are all over the place and I'd like to go there just to pick up on the vibrations.[467]

*

I enjoyed Japan a great deal when I was there, particularly the Rinzai Zen temples in Kyoto. I came away from a day and a half of Zen rock gardens floating on a sea of serenity that lasted two weeks. But I did realize one thing: basically, every country averages out to about the same thing. If there's more grace and aesthetic sense, perhaps there's less individuality. Like that.[468]

*

I think we're all here for the same purpose. There's a zen master who addressed his crowd as bodhisattvas, meaning everybody's come back just to show the way. Everybody is here to show the way, so there's no difference among us, there's no karmic scaling here, there's no better or worse, you know.[469]

*

As far as I get it, Zen is about facing life without carrying around a particular agenda. Perhaps it might help you make your case without getting too excited about it, which may be as far as it can go.

One other thing: I am totally sure that Zen does not tell us to put up with any and everything that comes our way. I believe instead that the hope and idea is to do what must be done, including fighting for our human rights and needs, but without going into the blame game. Doing what we have to do with a will and with best wishes for all involved. I think Jesus meant something like this, too, when he said love your enemies.[470]

*

Actually, meditation is only concentrated thinking on one subject. But that thinking must be sincere and with no distracting noises or bothersome things to ruin your peace and quiet.

Let's say you use a candle flame to concentrate on, as I do sometimes. Maybe you like to have some sweet, fragrant incense burning. Sit comfortably and decide on what you want to meditate about.

Now when you meditate, allow your mind to settle. Try not to let questions like, "Am I really meditating? Am I doing this right?" bother you. Instead relax, let your mind settle on whatever you're meditating about, and let your subject of meditation fill your mind.

You can meditate on anything! The trees, a tree, and their shapes and colors against the sky. Or on the sky itself and its deep blue. Whatever you see around you, or whoever is in your life, all these things are good subject for your meditation. And there are other, more abstract subjects as well, such as love itself, which is almost a life-time study, and such as how things go together, if at all.

Man was born with the freedom to be happy naturally. If you're unhappy, that's a clue your inner mind is giving you, telling you to root out the lies you've bought, telling you to shuck your chains. By learning to meditate, you can finally see what's making you unhappy, and get rid of it all!

Actually your whole life and your whole world is right in the corner of your head right now. All you need to do is to find the pathway to it, the pathway to the truth about yourself.

Some people say it isn't good to learn the truth about yourself, because the truth hurts! That may seem to be the way things are, but that's not really where it's at. I think you'll agree: truth and God mean the same thing. God and love meant the same thing. So

Love is the Truth and vice versa. And how can Love, or God, hurt you? It's not the truth that hurts, no. It's the shock of knowing that you've lived with a lie about yourself for a long, long time that really hurts you. Meditation can fix all that.

Micky once said it like this: In a way, we are all like trees. The parts of us that are above ground, the part of our minds that other people see everyday, are like a tree's limbs and leaves. But there's just as much to our inner mind as a tree has roots under the ground, just as many roots as it has limbs and branches. You have your own worth inside of your own head. And your roots of meditation are reaching deep, deep down into that earth for spiritual understanding of yourself. When you meditate, you're tracing those roots down, running along inside them to see where they go and what secrets about you they've found deep in the rich depths of that earth that's inside your head.

When you meditate with peace and love, and after you've done it for a while and learned how it has to work, just for you, you will start to get "flashes" in your mind! You've probably all had some already, which only goes to show how natural meditation is. They will be super out-a-site ideas that you'll all of a sudden understand about yourself and about life and about the love that really runs all though your life. And you'll say to yourself, "Hey! I knew that all the time!" And you know what? You did know it all the time! You've known it deep down in your inner mind ever since you were the littlest baby! Because that's the real you! The only reason you never thought about that secret from the inner you before is that you just never reached deep down for it before, down deep into your inner mind by meditation!

Life is a big puzzle. And you know you can put the pieces together, if you can just figure out the way to start.

Meditation is the way.

Peace.[471]

*

When I was in junior high school, I was a punk. I wanted people to love and admire me for my gentle wit, my talented music-making and my beauty of personality. Instead I was loathsome and irritating and quarrelsome and I didn't know why people didn't like me.

But I began to think and meditate on it. Meditation is the only way the personality can be improved, and gradually I began to work things out and better myself.

I like to give someone as many "different sheets of music paper" as I can — behave differently toward him each time I see him. That is the only way someone can know what the real me is like. You can't know the real me by only talking to me. I believe that you can tell more about people by the way they look walking away from you than you can by what they say.[472]

*

Zen also teaches that you should just go along and live your life as best you can from minute to minute, always living in the present. You're already there and there's nothing else. If you can make the most of each day, accomplish and learn all you can *now*, you'll get so much more done in your lifetime than if you sit around waiting for tomorrow to come. Because when *tomorrow* gets here it's just another *today*. You end up just waiting and putting things off and nothing ever gets done. So, try to make each minute count![473]

Tork About Zhe End...

September, 2018

Well, the experimental thing didn't work. I'm just going to stop all treatment.

[Am I sure?] Yeah, I don't want to stick around if I can't be amused. If I can't have fun, why would I stick around?[474]

It means that I have three to nine months. It means that I hope I make Christmas.

*

Christmas Day, 2018

Well, now I'm shootin' for my birthday…[475]

*

February 19, 2019 — Six days after his 77th birthday

I'm just waiting…[476]

*

February 21, 2019

Peter Tork passed away peacefully at home

Well, so what? Let's laugh 'til the end.[477]

Acknowledgements

The author would like to personally thank the following people for their support and assistance in getting the wise words of Peter Tork from his mouth and into your hands. We sincerely hope you, the reader, will benefit from them.

Harold Bronson, Steve Escobar, Ann Hackler, Brian Hiatt, Therra Cathryn Gwyn, Susan Klein, Dave Lefkowitz and the Dave's Gone By radio show, Monty Meyer and Take 12 Recovery Radio, June Millington, Ken Mills and Zilch A Monkees Podcast, Bruce Polluck, James Lee Stanley, and the REAL Peter Tork (Official) Facebook Page team.

I would also like to thank Peter, wherever you may be, for taking the time to share your words in an attempt help any and all fellow souls make their way through this dense human experience. It is my hope that this book will continue to allow your words to inspire others.

Tork About Zhe End...

References

[1] Rosen, T, "In The Mind Of...", *INTHEMINDOFTV*, YouTube, 7 May 2010

[2] Gwyn, TC, "Ask Peter Tork", *The Daily Panic*, 2009

[3] Gwyn, TC, "Ask Peter Tork", *The Daily Panic*, 2008

[4] Gwyn, TC, "Ask Peter Tork", *The Daily Panic*, 2008

[5] Gwyn, TC, "Ask Peter Tork", *The Daily Panic*, 2009

[6] Gwyn, TC, "Ask Peter Tork", *The Daily Panic*, 2009

[7] Gwyn, TC, "Ask Peter Tork", *The Daily Panic*, 2008

[8] Gwyn, TC, "Ask Peter Tork", *The Daily Panic*, 2008

[9] *WGLD Radio*, 1999

[10] "Peter Sez", *The REAL Peter Tork (Official) Facebook Page*, 2014

[11] Gwyn, TC, "Ask Peter Tork", *The Daily Panic*, September 2010

[12] Meyer, M, *Take 12 Recovery Radio*, www.Take12Radio.com, 2008

[13] "Sobriety Talks", Audio Recording, 1997

[14] Meyer, M, *Take 12 Recovery Radio*, www.Take12Radio.com, 2008

[15] Lefcowitz, E, Interview, 1983

[16] Polluck, B, *When The Music Mattered: Portraits From The 1960's*, 2011

[17] Polluck, B, *When The Music Mattered: Portraits From The 1960's*, 2011

[18] "Sobriety Talks", Audio Recording, 1997

[19] Recovery Fest, Glen Allen VA, 12 September 2009

[20] Meyer, M, *Take 12 Recovery Radio*, www.Take12Radio.com, 2008

[21] "Sobriety Talks", Audio Recording, 1997

[22] "Sobriety Talks", Audio Recording, 1997

[23] Escobar, S, "Peter Tork Off The Record", *www.steve-escobar.com/peter-tork*

[24] Gwyn, TC, "Ask Peter Tork", *The Daily Panic*, 2008

[25] Hiatt, B, "Peter Tork, A Lost Tell-All Interview On His Glory Years", 2007

[26] Escobar, S, "Peter Tork Off The Record", *www.steve-escobar.com/peter-tork*

[27] Fitzgerald, J, *The Gazette*, 27 May 1982

[28] "Peter Sez", *The REAL Peter Tork (Official) Facebook Page*, 3 January 2013

[29] Gwyn, TC, "Ask Peter Tork", *The Daily Panic*, 2008

30 Gwyn, TC, "Ask Peter Tork", *The Daily Panic*, 2008

31 Gwyn, TC, "Ask Peter Tork", *The Daily Panic*, 2009

32 Gwyn, TC, "Ask Peter Tork", *The Daily Panic*, 2008

33 Hulse, A, *Fave*, May 1968

34 "Peter Sez #37", *The REAL Peter Tork (Official) Facebook Page*, 17 January 2019

35 Mills, K, *Zilch A Monkees Podcast*, "#67 Peter Tork & Shoe Suede Blues", 2 September 2016

36 Gwyn, TC, "Ask Peter Tork", *The Daily Panic*, April 2008

37 Sullivan, A, "Peter Tork brings blues band to Secaucus", *The Secaucus Reporter*, 14 September 2003

38 Gwyn, TC, "Ask Peter Tork", *The Daily Panic*, March 2008

39 "Peter Sez #7", *The REAL Peter Tork (Official) Facebook Page*, 20 January 2012

40 Meyer, M, *Take 12 Recovery Radio*, www.Take12Radio.com, 2008

41 Hinckley, D, "Tork On Blues: I'm a believer", *NY Daily News*, 15 July 2003

42 Richmond, J, "Peter Talking on the Transatlantic Phone", *Monkees Monthly*, March 1968

43 *Fave*, March 1968

44 *Fave*, March 1968

45 Gwyn, TC, "Ask Peter Tork", *The Daily Panic*, 2008

46 *16 Magazine*, 1968

47 *16 Magazine*, February 1968

48 *The REAL Peter Tork (Official) Facebook Page*, 22 Feb 2019

49 "Sobriety Talks", Audio Recording, 1997

50 "Sobriety Talks", Audio Recording, 1997

51 *Music Groups*, 2007

52 *Seventeen*, August 1967

53 Iannoli, I, Untitled Documentary Project, 2015

54 "Sobriety Talks", Audio Recording, 1997

55 "Profiles, featuring Peter Tork", 7 April 2010

56 Baker, GA, *Monkeemania: The True Story of The Monkees*, 1 December 1986

57 *The Daily Oklahoman*, 7 November 1983

58 Baker, GA, *Monkeemania: The True Story of The Monkees*, 1 December 1986

59 Iannoli, I, Untitled Documentary Project, 2015

60 Stanley, JL, Author Interview, 18 July 2020

61 "Peter Sez #12", *The REAL Peter Tork (Official) Facebook Page*, 22 July 2012

62 Mills, K, Zilch A Monkees Podcast #67 Peter Tork & Shoe Suede Blues, 2 September 2016

63 Tardan, D, *Reasonably Spontaneous Conversation*, California Public Access TV, 1979

64 Tardan, D, *Reasonably Spontaneous Conversation*, California Public Access TV, 1979

65 Bronson, H, *Hey, Hey, We're The Monkees*, p. 15, 1996

66 Vivinetto, G, *Toking Heads: The Monkees Story*, 2000

67 Bronson, H, *Hey, Hey, We're The Monkees*, p. 94, 1996

68 *WNEW Radio*, 1982

69 Sandoval, A, *The Monkees: The Day-By-Day Story Of The 60s TV Pop Sensation*, 2005

70 *Thorkelson Thapes*, 9 November 1976

71 Richmond, J, "Peter Talking on the Transatlantic Phone", *Monkees Monthly*, March 1968

72 Bronson, H, *Hey, Hey, We're The Monkees*, p. 110, 1996

73 *The REAL Peter Tork (Official) Facebook Page*, 1 March 2012

74 *UK Music Reviews*, 28 May 2015

75 Goddard, S, *Oldies 92.7 - KAZG Radio*, July 2013

76 *Billboard*, 1 March 2012

77 *LeHigh Valley Live*, June 2012

78 "Why I Loved Davy Jones", *Savannah Morning News*, 7 March 2012,

79 *Boston Globe*, 16 May, 2013

80 "From Peter... regarding Rachel Maddow", *The REAL Peter Tork (Official) Facebook Page*, 4 March 2012

81 *Clevescene*, 13 March 2017

82 *Las Vegas Weekly*, 14 September 2016

83 Note to the Davy Jones Memorial, Beavertown, PA, 2012

84 "Peter Sez #12", *The REAL Peter Tork (Official) Facebook Page*, 22 July 2012

85 *Fave*, March 1968

86 Yonke, D, *Toledo Blade*, 5 November 2009

87 Rosen, T, "In The Mind Of...", INTHEMINDOFTV, YouTube, 7 May 2010

88 Polluck, B, *When The Music Mattered: Portraits From The 1960's*, 2011

89 Stanley, JL, "Peter Tork Interview", *Datamusicata*

90 Recovery Fest, Glen Allen VA, 12 September 2009

91 Gwyn, TC, "Ask Peter Tork", *The Daily Panic*, February 2008

92 Gwyn, TC, "Ask Peter Tork", *The Daily Panic*, 2009

93 Gwyn, TC, "Ask Peter Tork", *The Daily Panic*, 2009

94 Hulse, A, *Fave*, April 1968

95 Hiatt, B, "Peter Tork, A Lost Tell-All Interview On His Glory Years", 2007

96 Gwyn, TC, "Ask Peter Tork", *The Daily Panic*, Jul 2008

97 "Peter Tork Live at the Speakeasy", *Youtube*, 26 Nov 1988

98 Southworth, J, *Fabulous 208*, 17 January 1968

99 Tardan, D, *Reasonably Spontaneous Conversation*, California Public Access TV, 1979

100 "In This Generation", Live Show, 2013

101 Southworth, J, *Fabulous 208*, 17 January 1968

102 Baker, GA, *Monkeemania: The True Story of The Monkees*, 1 December 1986

103 *MPR*, 1987

104 Gwyn, TC, "Ask Peter Tork", *The Daily Panic*, 2008

105 Overbearing, L, "A Hostile Poolside Interview", *Hullabaloo*, September 1967

106 *The Cincinnati Enquirer*, 7 January 1967

107 *Seventeen*, August 1967

108 *Goldmine*, 1982

109 *Headquarters Radio*, September 1989

110 *The Journal Times Online*, 12 August 2005

111 *Thorkelson Thapes*, 9 November 1976

112 *KTRU*, 28 August 1983

113 *Hullabaloo*, February 1968

114 LaRue Huget, J, "Peter Tork's Cancer In His Own Words", *Washington Post*, 1 July 2009

115 "The Monkee who sings better than ever because he had throat cancer", *Daily Mail*, 16 August 2011

116 Gwyn, TC, "Ask Peter Tork", *The Daily Panic*, July 2010

117 "Monkee Peter Tork Not Letting Cancer Stop Him From Performing", *Antimusic*, 27 May 2009

118 "A Note of Thanks from Peter to his Fans", *The REAL Peter Tork (Official) Facebook Page*, 13 February 2012

119 Gwyn, TC, "Ask Peter Tork", *The Daily Panic*, 2008

120 Polluck, B, *When The Music Mattered: Portraits From The 1960's*, 2011

121 Iannoli, I, Untitled Documentary Project, 2015

122 Gwyn, TC, "Ask Peter Tork", *The Daily Panic*, April 2008

123 *Flip*, August 1967

124 *Seventeen*, August 1967

125 Gwyn, TC, "Ask Peter Tork", *The Daily Panic*, 2008

126 Stavers, G, *16 Magazine*, September 1968

127 *Creem Presents...*, "The Monkees: Yesterday, Today & Tomorrow", April 1987

128 "Peter Sez #21", *The REAL Peter Tork (Official) Facebook Page*, 30 March 2014

129 Gwyn, TC, "Ask Peter Tork", *The Daily Panic*, 2008

130 Gwyn, TC, "Ask Peter Tork", *The Daily Panic*, 2008

131 Hiatt, B, "Peter Tork, A Lost Tell-All Interview On His Glory Years", 2007

132 Polluck, B, *When The Music Mattered: Portraits From The 1960's*, 2011

133 Rosen, T, "In The Mind Of...", *INTHEMINDOFTV*, YouTube, 7 May 2010

134 Gwyn, TC, "Ask Peter Tork", *The Daily Panic*, March 2008

135 Sims, J, *Disc & Music Echo*

136 Polluck, B, *When The Music Mattered: Portraits From The 1960's*, 2011

137 Mills, K, *Zilch A Monkees Podcast*, "#67 Peter Tork & Shoe Suede Blues", 2 September 2016

138 Mills, K, *Zilch A Monkees Podcast*, "#67 Peter Tork & Shoe Suede Blues", 2 September 2016

139 Mills, K, *Zilch A Monkees Podcast*, "#67 Peter Tork & Shoe Suede Blues", 2 September 2016

140 Rosen, T, "In The Mind Of...", *INTHEMINDOFTV*, YouTube, 7 May 2010

141 Elder, J, *Countdown*, April 1987

142 Stenza, L, *Connecticut Daily Campus*, 26 February 1982

143 The 1982 Monkees Convention

144 *My Generation with Leeza Gibbons*, 25 Mar 2011

145 Polluck, B, *When The Music Mattered: Portraits From The 1960's*, 2011

146 Hulse, A, *Fave*, April 1968

147 *Justus*, The Monkees, 1996

148 Gwyn, TC, "Ask Peter Tork", *The Daily Panic*, 2008

149 Gwyn, TC, "Ask Peter Tork", *The Daily Panic*, 2009

150 Gwyn, TC, "Ask Peter Tork", *The Daily Panic*, 2009

151 *KROQ-FM 106.7*, "Loveline with Dr Drew Pinsky", 1995

152 "Sobriety Talks", Audio Recording, 1997

153 *Clash Magazine*, 2012

154 Gwyn, TC, "Ask Peter Tork", *The Daily Panic*, 2009

155 *Monkee Spectacular*, No. 14, June 1968

156 Gwyn, TC, Author Interview

157 Polluck, B, *When The Music Mattered: Portraits From The 1960's*, 2011

158 *Visalia Times Delta*, 29 October 2010

159 Gwyn, TC, "Ask Peter Tork", *The Daily Panic*, April 2008

160 *The Boston Globe*, 10 August 1989

161 *WNEW*, 1982

162 *Teen Pin-Ups Magazine*, May 1967

163 Hulse, A, *Fave*, April 1968

164 *Disc & Music Echo*, 13 January 1968

165 Moses, A, *Tiger Beat*, April 1968

166 *Chicago Tribune*, 19 January 1996

167 *WDBB*, 12 February 2006

168 *The REAL Peter Tork (Official) Facebook Page*, 2014

169 *Good Times*, The Monkees, 2016

170 *Disc and Music Echo*, 13 January 1968

171 Polluck, B, *When The Music Mattered: Portraits From The 1960's*, 2011

172 Bronson, H, *Hey, Hey, We're The Monkees*, p.21, 1996

173 *Thorkelson Thapes*, 20 October 1976

174 Overbearing, L, "A Hostile Poolside Interview", *Hullabaloo*, September 1967

175 Bronson, H, *Hey, Hey, We're The Monkees*, p. 28, 1996

176 "Peter Tork Answers Your Questions", *Flip*, August 1967

177 *Clevescene*, 13 March 2017

178 DVD commentary, "Daydream Believers, The Monkees Story", 2000

179 Escobar, S, "Peter Tork Off The Record", *www.steve-escobar.com/peter-tork*

180 Bronson, H, *Hey, Hey, We're The Monkees*, p. 129, 1996

181 *Thorkelson Thapes*, 30 January 1977

182 *Thorkelson Thapes*, 9 November 1976

183 *Thorkelson Thapes*, 9 November 1976

184 DVD commentary, "Daydream Believers, The Monkees Story", 2000

185 *The Republican*, 16 March 2001

186 Bloom, S, "Peter Tork, Still Baffled By 'Head', 'When Do We Get Out Of The Box?'", *Hollywood Reporter*, 30 July 2013

187 Lee, I, Interview, 2012

188 Bronson, H, *Hey, Hey, We're The Monkees*, p.94, 1996

189 Benner, R, *Monkee Spectacular*, April 1968

190 Bronson, H, *Hey, Hey, We're The Monkees*, p.28, 1996

191 Bronson, H, *Hey, Hey, We're The Monkees*, p.136, 1996

192 "Peter Tork Answers Your Questions", *Flip*, August 1967

193 Benner, R, *Monkee Spectacular*, April 1968

194 *Thorkelson Thapes*, 9 November 1976

195 Overbearing, L, "A Hostile Poolside Interview", *Hullabaloo*, September 1967

196 DVD commentary, "Daydream Believers, The Monkees Story", 2000

197 *The Monkees Music Box*, "Disc 2 Album Liner Notes", 2001

198 Bronson, H, *Hey, Hey, We're The Monkees*, p.132, 1996

199 Sandoval, A, Interview, 2005

200 Mills, K, *Zilch A Monkees Podcast*, "#67 Peter Tork & Shoe Suede Blues", 2 September 2016

201 *Clevescene*, 13 March 2017

202 Bronson, H, *Hey, Hey, We're The Monkees*, p.94, 1996

203 *BBC WM*, 2015

204 Gaar, G, "What Did You Expect Me To Say", *Rock and Roll Globe*, 2016

205 Gwyn, TC, "Ask Peter Tork", *The Daily Panic*, September 2010

206 Richmond, J, "Peter Talking on the Transatlantic Phone", *Monkees Monthly*, March 1968

207 *Disc and Music Echo*, 20 January 1968

208 Bronson, H, *Hey, Hey, We're The Monkees*, p. 89, 1996

209 Das, L, "Sex, Drugs, and a Lot of Monkee Business", *Weekend*, 19 August 2015

210 Polluck, B, *When The Music Mattered: Portraits From The 1960's*, 2011

211 *New West*, 1 January 1979

212 *Goldmine*, 1982

213 Polluck, B, *When The Music Mattered: Portraits From The 1960's*, 2011

214 *GOLD 104.5*, 1999

215 Tardan, D, *Reasonably Spontaneous Conversation*, California Public Access TV, 1979

216 Gwyn, TC, *Ask Peter Tork*, The Daily Panic, March 2008

217 *The Rock Island Argus*, 15 August 1996

218 Stenza, L, *Connecticut Daily Campus*, 26 February 1982

219 Berlin, J, *Toxic Fame: Celebrities Speak on Stardom*, 1 May 1996

220 Du Lac, F, *Commonwealth Reporter*, June 1969

[221] Vivinetto, G, "Toking Heads, The Monkees Story", 27 September 2005

[222] "In This Generation", Live Show, 2013

[223] "In This Generation", Live Show, 2013

[224] *The News and Observer*, 13 September 2004

[225] DVD commentary, "Daydream Believers, The Monkees Story", 2000

[226] *Bohemian*, 2002

[227] "From Peter... Regarding Rachel Maddow," *The REAL Peter Tork (Official) Facebook Page*, 4 March 2012

[228] Rosen, T, "In The Mind Of...", *INTHEMINDOFTV*, YouTube, 7 May 2010

[229] *MOJO*, June 2002

[230] *Blitz!*, May/June 1980

[231] Gwyn, TC, "Ask Peter Tork", *The Daily Panic*, 2009

[232] Wilson, KM, *Leo Weekly*, 8 June 2016

[233] Gwyn, TC, "Ask Peter Tork", *The Daily Panic*, 2008

[234] *WNEW*, 1982

[235] *WGLD RADIO*

[236] *NPR Fresh Air*, June 3, 1983

237 Polluck, B, *When The Music Mattered: Portraits From The 1960's*, 2011

238 *Pisces, Aquarius, Capricorn & Jones Ltd.*, "Liner Notes", 2007

239 *Arizona Republic*, 5 April 2001

240 *Guitar World*, 26 July 2013

241 *Guitar World*, 26 July 2013

242 *Headquarters Radio*, September 1989

243 Fitzgerald, J, *The Gazette*, 27 May 1982

244 DVD commentary, "Daydream Believers, The Monkees Story", 2000

245 *WNEW*, 1982

246 *NZ Herald*, 25 Nov 2016

247 *Rolling Stone*, 7 March 2011

248 Das, L, "Sex, Drugs, and a Lot of Monkee Business", *Weekend*, 19 August 2015

249 *Poughkeepsie Journal*, 30 January 2004

250 *The Plain Dealer*, 7 June 1986

251 *Review Magazine*, 27 May 2016

252 *The REAL Peter Tork (Official) Facebook Page*, 27 March 2015

253 *Phawker*, 2012

254 DVD commentary, "Daydream Believers, The Monkees Story", 2000

255 Lefcowics, E, Interview 1983

256 Polluck, B, *When The Music Mattered: Portraits From The 1960's*, 2011

257 *Los Angeles Times*, 12 November 1995

258 *Citizens' Voice*, 19 October 1983

259 *Seventeen*, August 1967

260 *Thorkelson Thapes*, 1 November 1976

261 Meyer, M, *Take 12 Recovery Radio*, www.Take12Radio.com, 2008

262 *Headquarters Radio*, 1989

263 *Guitar Player Magazine*, October 2016

264 *Headquarters*, "Liner Notes", 1995

265 Gwyn, TC, "Ask Peter Tork", *The Daily Panic*, April 2008

266 Gwyn, TC, "Ask Peter Tork", *The Daily Panic*, February 2008

267 Cott, J

268 "Peter Sez #6," *The REAL Peter Tork (Official) Facebook Page*, 4 December 2011

269 Gwyn, TC, "Ask Peter Tork", *The Daily Panic*, 2008

270 Gwyn, TC, "Ask Peter Tork", *The Daily Panic*, April 2008

271 "Peter Sez", *The REAL Peter Tork (Official) Facebook Page*

272 Gwyn, TC, "Ask Peter Tork", *The Daily Panic*, 2008

273 Gwyn, TC, "Ask Peter Tork", *The Daily Panic*, Sep 2008

274 *Review Magazine*, 27 May 2016

275 DVD commentary, "Daydream Believers, The Monkees Story", 2000

276 *MLive*, 21 August 2012

277 "Moderato ma non troppo, performed live", *Peter Tork Bandcamp*, 10 March 2015

278 Hiatt, B, "Peter Tork, A Lost Tell-All Interview On His Glory Years", 2007

279 Mills, K, *Zilch A Monkees Podcast*, "#67 Peter Tork & Shoe Suede Blues", 2 September 2016

280 Rosen, T, "In The Mind Of...", *INTHEMINDOFTV*, YouTube, 7 May 2010

281 *Enigma Online*, 5 November 2015

282 Gwyn, TC, "Ask Peter Tork", *The Daily Panic*, 2009

283 Gwyn, TC, "Ask Peter Tork", *The Daily Panic*, July 2010

284 Gwyn, TC, "Ask Peter Tork", *The Daily Panic*

[285] *Evening Standard*, 26 July 1983

[286] *VH1*, 1988

[287] Lefkowitz, D, *Daves Gone By*, Radio Interview, TotalTheatre Productions, 12 February 2006

[288] "The Monkee who sings better than ever because he had throat cancer", *Daily Mail*, 16 August 2011

[289] "Sobriety Talks", Audio Recording, 1997

[290] *Together*, November/December 2010

[291] *Teen Magazine*, 1968

[292] *Tiger Beat*, September 1967

[293] Gwyn, TC, "Ask Peter Tork", *The Daily Panic*

[294] Gwyn, TC, "Ask Peter Tork", *The Daily Panic*

[295] Stone, J, *The New York Times*, 2 October 1966

[296] Gwyn, TC, "Ask Peter Tork", *The Daily Panic*

[297] *The REAL Peter Tork (Official) Facebook Page*, 11 September 2011

[298] Gwyn, TC, "Ask Peter Tork", *The Daily Panic*

[299] *Together*, November/December 2010

[300] Goddard, S, *Oldies 92.7 KAZG Radio*, July 2013,

[301] *Monkee Spectacular*, June 1968

302 *DGB*, 12 February 2006

303 *American Girl*, October 1967

304 Tardan, D, *Reasonably Spontaneous Conversation*, California Public Access TV, 1979

305 Richmond, J, "Peter Talking on the Transatlantic Phone", *Monkees Monthly*, March 1968

306 *The Making of Justus*, Documentary, 1996

307 *This Is Derbyshire*, 16 May 2008

308 Rosen, T, "In The Mind Of...", *INTHEMINDOFTV*, YouTube, 7 May 2010

309 Iannoli, I, Untitled Documentary Project, 2015

310 Overbearing, L, "A Hostile Poolside Interview", *Hullabaloo*, September 1967

311 Baker, GA, *Monkeemania: The True Story of The Monkees*, 1 December 1986

312 *Blitz!*, May/June 1980

313 "Peter Sez #24", *The REAL Peter Tork (Official) Facebook Page*, 24 December 2014

314 "Peter Sez #5", *The REAL Peter Tork (Official) Facebook Page*, 24 November 2011

315 Rosen, T, "In The Mind Of...", *INTHEMINDOFTV*, YouTube, 7 May 2010

316 Rosen, T, "In The Mind Of...", *INTHEMINDOFTV*, YouTube, 7 May 2010

317 Gwyn, TC, "Ask Peter Tork", *The Daily Panic*, September 2010

318 Rosen, T, "In The Mind Of...", *INTHEMINDOFTV*, YouTube, 7 May 2010

319 Rosen, T, "In The Mind Of...", *INTHEMINDOFTV*, YouTube, 7 May 2010

320 "Peter Sez #3", The REAL Peter Tork (Official) Facebook Page, 31 October 2011

321 Overbearing, L, "A Hostile Poolside Interview", *Hullabaloo*, September 1967

322 Rosen, T, "In The Mind Of...", *INTHEMINDOFTV*, YouTube, 7 May 2010

323 Meyer, M, *Take 12 Recovery Radio*, www.Take12Radio.com, 2008

324 *KTRU*, August 1983

325 *KROQ-FM 106.7*, "Loveline with Dr Drew Pinsky", 1995

326 *Medium*, 2017

327 *NPR Fresh Air*, 3 June 1983

328 *Music Groups*, 2007

329 Zielinski, M, *The Gazette*, 31 October 1986

330 Gwyn, TC, "Ask Peter Tork", *The Daily Panic*, July 2008

331 Rosen, T, "In The Mind Of...", *INTHEMINDOFTV*, YouTube, 7 May 2010

332 *KLOS Radio*, "Breakfast With The Beatles", 16 June 2013

333 "Peter Sez #31", *The REAL Peter Tork (Official) Facebook Page*, 14 March 2021

334 Moses, A, *Monkee Spectacular*, November 1967

335 "Peter Sez #17", *The REAL Peter Tork (Official) Facebook Page*, 12 June 2013

336 Rosen, T, "In The Mind Of...", *INTHEMINDOFTV*, YouTube, 7 May 2010

337 *LeHigh Valley Live*, 2012

338 Fitzgerald, J, *The Gazette*, 27 May 1982

339 *16 Magazine*, 16 December 1968

340 Stavers, G, *16 Magazine*, December 1968

341 "Peter Tork Answers Your Questions", *Flip*, August 1967

342 Gwyn, TC, "Ask Peter Tork", *The Daily Panic*, 2008

343 Taylor, T, *Teen Life*, "I'm Going Into Politics", August 1967

344 Lefcowitz, E, Interview 1983

345 *NPR Fresh Air*, 3 June 1983

346 Gwyn, TC, "Ask Peter Tork", *The Daily Panic*, 2009

347 Gwyn, TC, "Ask Peter Tork", *The Daily Panic*, 2009

348 Rosen, T, "In The Mind Of...", INTHEMINDOFTV, YouTube, 7 May 2010

349 *The Age*, September 18, 1968

350 United Fan Convention Q&A, November 2006

351 Polluck, B, *When The Music Mattered: Portraits From The 1960's*, 2011

352 Hiatt, B, "Peter Tork, A Lost Tell-All Interview On His Glory Years", 2007

353 The 1989 Monkees Convention Q&A, 1989

354 Gwyn, TC, "Ask Peter Tork", *The Daily Panic*, 2010

355 Holdship, B, *Creem Presents Magazine,* April 1987

356 Gwyn, TC, "Ask Peter Tork", *The Daily Panic*, September 2010

357 Gwyn, TC, "Ask Peter Tork", *The Daily Panic*, July 2010

358 Gwyn, TC, "Ask Peter Tork", *The Daily Panic*, April 2008

359 Rosen, T, "In The Mind Of...", INTHEMINDOFTV, YouTube, 7 May 2010

360 Falkenberg, LL, "Interview with Peter Tork", 1994

361 Polluck, B, *When The Music Mattered: Portraits From The 1960's*, 2011

362 "Peter Sez #19", *The REAL Peter Tork (Official) Facebook Page*, 13 November 2013

363 "Peter Sez" *The REAL Peter Tork (Official) Facebook Page*, 31 December 2011

364 *The Daily Journal*, 21 October 2009

365 Gwyn, TC, "Ask Peter Tork", *The Daily Panic*, 2008

366 *Together*, November/December 2010

367 *Florida Today*, 10 May 10 2016

368 *Thorkelson Thapes*, 14 October 1976

369 Stanley, JL, *Datamusicata*, "Peter Tork Interview", 4 September 2007

370 Cooper, K, "Interview: Peter Tork", *UK Music Reviews*

371 "Peter Tork - Good Looker Live in Milwaukee WI 5-04-98", *Sunnygirlfriend13*, Youtube, 5 April 1998

372 *Thorkelson Thapes*, 29 November 1976

373 Gwyn, TC, "Ask Peter Tork", *The Daily Panic*, February 2008

374 Gwyn, TC, "Ask Peter Tork", *The Daily Panic*, February 2008

375 Gwyn, TC, "Ask Peter Tork", *The Daily Panic*, March 2008

376 Gwyn, TC, "Ask Peter Tork", *The Daily Panic*, 2008

377 *KROQ-FM 106.7, "Loveline with Dr Drew Pinsky", 1995*

378 "Sobriety Talks", Audio Recording, 1997

379 Gwyn, TC, "Ask Peter Tork", *The Daily Panic*, February 2008

380 Gwyn, TC, "Ask Peter Tork", *The Daily Panic*, 2008

381 Gwyn, TC, "Ask Peter Tork", *The Daily Panic*, September 2010

382 Gwyn, TC, "Ask Peter Tork", *The Daily Panic*, April 2008

383 *WFAN-FM*, 24 November 24 2009

384 Des Barres, P, *Rock Bottom: Dark Moments in Music Babylon*, 1995

385 Hiatt, B, "Peter Tork, A Lost Tell-All Interview On His Glory Years", 2007

386 *KROQ-FM 106.7, "Loveline with Dr Drew Pinsky", 1995*

387 Gwyn, TC, "Ask Peter Tork", *The Daily Panic*, 2008

388 Polluck, B, *When The Music Mattered: Portraits From The 1960's*, 2011

389 Gwyn, TC, "Peter Tork Explains It All For You", *Arts In America*, 13 February 2010

390 *Monkee Spectacular*, No. 14, June 1968

391 Tardan, D, *Reasonably Spontaneous Conversation*, California Public Access TV, 1979

392 Berlin, J, *Toxic Fame: Celebrities Speak on Stardom,* 1 May 1996

393 *The Daily Oklahoman,* 7 November 1983

394 Gwyn, TC, "Ask Peter Tork", *The Daily Panic,* Jul 2008

395 Gwyn, TC, "Ask Peter Tork", *The Daily Panic,* March 2008

396 *Fave,* 1969

397 Gwyn, TC, "Ask Peter Tork", *The Daily Panic,* 2008

398 Woliver, R, *Bringing It All Back Home: 25 Years of American Music at Folk City,* 1986

399 Bronson, H, *Hey, Hey, We're The Monkees,* p. 21, 1996

400 This Week In Grooviness, 2011

401 Gwyn, TC, "Ask Peter Tork", *The Daily Panic,* March 2008

402 Polluck, B, *When The Music Mattered: Portraits From The 1960's,* 2011

403 "Peter Sez #9", *The REAL Peter Tork (Official) Facebook Page,* 19 March 2012

404 *Asbury Park Press,* 9 July 1999

405 Polluck, B, *When The Music Mattered: Portraits From The 1960's,* 2011

406 Polluck, B, *When The Music Mattered: Portraits From The 1960's,* 2011

407 *Review Magazine*, May 2016

408 *Headquarters Radio*, September 1989

409 Gwyn, TC, "Ask Peter Tork", *The Daily Panic*, 2008

410 *KLOS Radio*, "Breakfast With The Beatles", 16 June 2013

411 *The Guardian*, 23 March 2017

412 Gwyn, TC, "Ask Peter Tork", *The Daily Panic*

413 Email response to The Adult Drug Court Graduation, 2010

414 Gwyn, TC, "Ask Peter Tork", *The Daily Panic*, April 2008

415 "Sobriety Talks", Audio Recording, 1997

416 Gwyn, TC, "Ask Peter Tork", *The Daily Panic*, April 2008

417 Berlin, J, *Toxic Fame: Celebrities Speak on Stardom*, 1 May 1996

418 Recovery Fest, Glen Allen VA, 12 September 2009

419 "Sobriety Talks", Audio Recording, 1997

420 *The Rik Turner Show*, January 1994

421 Recovery Fest, Glen Allen VA, 12 September 2009

422 Lefkowitz, D, *Daves Gone By*, Radio Interview, TotalTheatre Productions, 15 April 2007

423 Recovery Fest, Glen Allen VA, 12 September 2009

424 Gwyn, TC, "Ask Peter Tork", *The Daily Panic*, April 2008

425 Gwyn, TC, "Ask Peter Tork", *The Daily Panic*

426 Gwyn, TC, "Ask Peter Tork", *The Daily Panic*, 2009

427 "Sobriety Talks", Audio Recording, 1997

428 *KROQ-FM 106.7, "Loveline with Dr Drew Pinsky", 1995*

429 Gwyn, TC, "Ask Peter Tork", *The Daily Panic*, July 2008

430 Escobar, S, "Peter Tork Off The Record", *www.steve-escobar.com/peter-tork*

431 Gwyn, TC, "Ask Peter Tork", *The Daily Panic*, 2008

432 Gwyn, TC, "Ask Peter Tork", *The Daily Panic*, February 2008

433 Gwyn, TC, "Ask Peter Tork", *The Daily Panic*, April 2008

434 Lefkowitz, D, *Daves Gone By*, Radio Interview, TotalTheatre Productions, 15 April 2007

435 "Sobriety Talks", Audio Recording, 1997

436 Polluck, B, *When The Music Mattered: Portraits From The 1960's*, 2011

437 *KROQ-FM 106.7, "Loveline with Dr Drew Pinsky", 1995*

438 Cotton, C, *Fave*, March 1968

439 Radel, C, *The Cincinnati Enquirer*, 20 October 1983

440 Gwyn, TC, "Ask Peter Tork", *The Daily Panic*, July 2010

441 Benner, R, *Monkee Spectacular,* April 1968

442 Moses, A, *Tiger Beat Magazine,* April 1968

443 *Thorkelson Thapes,* 20 October 1976

444 Gwyn, TC, "Ask Peter Tork", *The Daily Panic,* September 2010

445 *16 Magazine,* 1968

446 Unknown

447 Bronson, H, *Hey, Hey, We're The Monkees,* p.144, 1996

448 "Peter Sez #27", *The REAL Peter Tork (Official) Facebook Page,* 16 December 2015

449 Rosen, T, "In The Mind Of…", *INTHEMINDOFTV,* YouTube, 7 May 2010

450 Tardan, D, *Reasonably Spontaneous Conversation,* California Public Access TV, 1979

451 *The Boston Globe,* 10 August 1989

452 *Seventeen,* August 1967

453 Stavers, G, *16 Magazine,* December 1968

454 Recovery Fest, Glen Allen VA, 12 September 2009

455 Mills, K, *Zilch A Monkees Podcast,* "#67 Peter Tork & Shoe Suede Blues", 2 September 2016

456 *Monkee Spectacular,* June 1968

457 Gwyn, TC, "Ask Peter Tork", *The Daily Panic*, 2009

458 Gwyn, TC, "Ask Peter Tork", *The Daily Panic*

459 Rosen, T, "In The Mind Of...", *INTHEMINDOFTV*, YouTube, 7 May 2010

460 Gwyn, TC, "Ask Peter Tork", *The Daily Panic*, April 2008

461 Dutton, C, *Chorley Citizen*, 23 May 23 2008

462 *Podcasting With... Todd and Dave*, 13 October 2010

463 Rosen, T, "In The Mind Of...", *INTHEMINDOFTV*, YouTube, 7 May 2010

464 *Los Angeles Times*, 20 October 1992

465 "Peter Sez #36", *The REAL Peter Tork (Official) Facebook Page*

466 Cotton, C, *Fave*, March 1968

467 "Peter Grooves on Japan", *Monkee Spectactular*, March 1968

468 Unknown

469 Unknown

470 Gwyn, TC, "Ask Peter Tork", *The Daily Panic*, 2008

471 Burgess, P, *Fave*, June 1968

472 *Seventeen*, August 1967

473 Cotton, C, *Fave*, March 1968

[474] Stanley, JL, Author Interview, 2020

[475] Stanley, JL, Author Interview, 2020

[476] Stanley, JL, Author Interview, 2020

[477] Millington, J, Author Interview, 2020

www.ingramcontent.com/pod-product-compliance
Lightning Source LLC
Chambersburg PA
CBHW020416010526
44118CB00010B/277